The Law of Parks
and
Open Spaces

Paul Clayden

Shaw & Sons

Shaw's
Since 1750

Published by
Shaw & Sons Limited
Shaway House
21 Bourne Park
Bourne Road
Crayford
Kent DA1 4BZ

www.shaws.co.uk

© Shaw & Sons Limited 2009

Published March 2009

ISBN 978 0 7219 0552 5

A CIP catalogue record for this book is
available from the British Library

Printed and bound in the UK by
CPI Antony Rowe, Chippenham, Wiltshire

THE LAW OF PARKS AND OPEN SPACES

Other books by Paul Clayden and published by Shaw & Sons:

The Councillor
The Dog Law Handbook
The Law of Allotments
The Law of Mobile Homes and Caravans
The Local Council Clerk's Guide
The Parish Councillor's Guide
Street Use and the Law

Contents

Contents

Contents

Contents

Contents

PREFACE

This book is the successor to *The Law of Parks and Recreation Grounds* by Roland Roddis, first published by Shaw & Sons in 1953 and of which a fourth and final edition was published in 1974. Since then, the law has in many respects changed greatly and on this ground alone a further edition of the book would not be justified. Since 1974, too, Shaw & Sons have published *Countryside Law* (the first edition was in 1987 and the fourth edition came out in 2004). *Countryside Law* covers a number of topics which were contained in Mr Roddis' book, namely access to the countryside, commons and village greens, country parks and the National Trust. This book does not therefore deal with these topics, save incidentally.

I am grateful to Michael Branaghan for his assistance in the drafting of Chapter 1.

Paul Clayden

TABLE OF STATUTES

Table of statutes

Table of statutes

Table of statutes

Table of statutes

TABLE OF STATUTORY INSTRUMENTS

TABLE OF CASES

DEFINITIONS

Assembly: the National Assembly for Wales.

Billing authority: the principal authority responsible for the levying and collection of council taxes and non-domestic rates.

Local authority: a local council, a principal council and a unitary council.

Local council: in England, a parish or town council; in Wales, a community or town council.

Principal council: in England, a county council, a district council, a unitary council, the Common Council of the City of London, the Council of the Isles of Scilly and a London borough council; in Wales, a county or county borough council.

Secretary of State: the Secretary of State for Communities and Local Government.

Unitary council: a district council for an area where there is no county council or a county council for an area for which there is no district council.

ABBREVIATIONS

CNEA 2005
Clean Neighbourhoods and Environment Act 2005.

DCLG
Department for Communities and Local Government.

DCMS
Department for Culture, Media and Sport.

DEFRA
Department for Environment, Food and Rural Affairs.

LGA 1972
Local Government Act 1972.

TCPA 1990
Town and Country Planning Act 1990.

Chapter 1

THE HISTORY OF PARKS AND OPEN SPACES

Introduction

Before the early nineteenth century, the English landscape was predominantly agricultural. Between 1700 and 1790, more than 1,620,000 hectares (4,000,000 acres) of common land and reclaimed land came under cultivation. Farmers introduced Dutch crop rotation techniques to increase yield. New technology and machinery, such as Jethro Tull's seed drill, revolutionised agricultural practices, creating less labour-intensive systems of work (*Briggs*[1]). The subsequent enclosure of common land by the landed gentry was seen as a necessary evil in 'improving agriculture'. As cities and towns began to expand, landowners found themselves in a highly lucrative position and able to substantially increase their wealth by feeding the growing urban population.

It was not until the nineteenth century that Victorian society witnessed the full extent of the radical urbanisation of the landscape and society. Urbanisation came as a direct result of an effective industrial evolution. Processes, which had previously been scattered within people's homes and workshops, were brought together on to one site (*Strong*[2]). The efficiencies that such an aggregation of trades and processes developed gave rise to the formation of industrial towns, in turn creating their own unique landscape and physical environment.

Victorian society welcomed the swift rise of industrialisation and the subsequent imperial expansion that paralleled such growth. Towns and cities grew at an alarming rate and to

1

such an extent that they engulfed the British countryside. Between 1821 and 1841 London grew by 20%; Manchester, Birmingham, Leeds and Sheffield by 40%; and Bradford by a staggering 65% (*Harrison*[3]).

Many historians see nineteenth century Britain's growing economy as the root cause of population growth in towns and cities (*Rubinstein*[4]). In the first half of the nineteenth century Britain's population had increased by 73%: a growth rate of two million people in each decade.

However, the growth of towns and cities was in stark contrast to the decline of the rural population, forced from traditional livelihoods by the enclosures. People drifted into towns and cities in an attempt to find better employment and higher wages. In 1800, 25% of the British population lived within towns or cities: by 1881 this had risen to 80% (*Strong*).

A lack of both formal development control and planning legislation resulted in the birth of inner-city ghettos, with back-to-back housing and airless tenement blocks. Such properties were often devoid of basic sanitation and subsequently this led to an increase in infant mortality through outbreaks of diseases such as cholera and typhoid. Between 1831 and 1866, there were four catastrophic cholera outbreaks within cities throughout the British Isles (*Hern*[5]).

As cities grew, between 1801 and 1851, municipal corporations were given the responsibility of dealing with health and public order pressures created as a consequence of industrialisation. Such responsibilities and powers of remedy were given by virtue of the Municipal Corporations Act 1835 and other legislation of the late nineteenth century (*Briggs*). The Reverend George Dawson, at that time, gave expression to municipality responsibilities when speaking of a ward meeting in Birmingham. He stated that:

> '[The discussion]...dwelt with growing enthusiasm on what a great and prosperous town like Birmingham might do for its people. They spoke of sweeping away streets in which it was not possible to live a healthy and decent life; of making the town cleaner, sweeter and brighter; of providing gardens and parks and music; or erecting baths and free libraries...' (*Gill*[6])

The extension of leisure to the majority of the urban workforce was a major social reform that was realised by 1850. Previously, leisure had been restricted to only a few fortunate people. From 1850, a pattern of working life had been established that created a five-and-a-half-day working week, with time off on Saturday afternoons and all day Sunday. Additionally, annual holidays were secured. The Bank Holiday Act 1871 established public holidays for Boxing Day, Easter Monday, Whit Monday and the first Monday in August. The first Bank Holiday under the Act occurred on 4th August 1871 (*Hern*).

The holiday concessions granted to the working classes generated considerable fears within the middle classes. People who had previously migrated from the countryside to towns and cities brought with them a number of pastimes such as cockfighting, bull-baiting and prize fighting. It was believed that these 'barbaric' pastimes would unleash unprecedented violent and anti-social behaviour (*Harrison*). As a consequence, fairs were suspended and opening hours restricted. In parallel to the restrictions imposed by the middle classes, 'rational recreation' was promoted. The theory suggested that time devoted to appropriate activities, such as the admiration of fine landscapes and paintings, was morally and spiritually

3

uplifting. It was argued that, by experiencing the cultured leisure environment sought after by the middle and upper classes, the urban poor would come to share such leisure tastes and moral values (*Harrison*).

Participation in team sports was seen as appropriate because it fostered a corporate spirit and proper behaviour. It was argued that time spent on appropriate leisure activities contributed:

> '...to a healthy and reliable workforce, to a fit and well-drilled defence force and to general improvement in moral standards and social behaviour.' (Cited in *Harrison*)

The development of formal parks and open spaces

The world's first municipal parks were created within the United Kingdom during the nineteenth century (*Conway*[7]). Until this time, park development was limited in number and extent (*Roger*[8]).

In 1833, the Government Select Committee on Public Walks presented a report to Parliament concerning the lack of open space availability for the labouring poor. The Committee recognised the benefits that could be derived from parks:

> '[Parks were]...the lungs for the city and would refresh the air; would improve people's health and provide places for exercise; would be an alternative form of recreation to the tavern; and would provide beneficial contact with nature, so elevating the spirit. Further more, as all members of society would use parks, social tensions would be reduced and classes would learn from each other.' (*Woudstra*[9])

From 1840, municipal parks were commissioned by the newly empowered municipal authorities, public subscription, benefactors and philanthropists – each unified in the belief that parks were a necessary development to deal with the social and economic evils arising through industrialisation and the subsequent growth of towns and cities (*Roger*).

Municipal parks were created on greens, commons, marginal land, old industrial sites and quarries. The characteristics of a site often influenced the design of the park (*Conway*). Some parks had previously been the grounds of large Victorian suburban houses. Ownership of such properties was transferred to local authorities in an attempt to avoid death duties and also to flee the encroachment of the suburbs (*Beresford*[10]).

Within every town and city, public parks were created in a formal style that represented a utilitarian approach to the use of open space. Many of the early designs were influenced by the work of Humphrey Repton, who had created private parks and pleasure grounds. A common aim of park design, at that time, was to develop a wide number of facilities and attractions within a landscape that would be capable of accommodating large numbers of people. As a result, a disciplined environment was created that ensured the playing of games, consumption of alcohol, playing of music or holding of meetings were prohibited or controlled by byelaws.

> 'The more we encourage Rational Recreation...the more we lessen sexual licence and its evil consequences, excessive alcohol consumption, the delight in immoral exhibitions, the admiration for torturing animals...and above all, the more we diminish the number of human beings that ponder to false pleasures...' (*Commission's Inquiry*[11])

The mid-nineteenth century brought with it a period of enlightenment. Educated people became aware that the earth and its wildlife had previously existed independently of human beings. People from all walks of life delighted in the diversity of nature. The inclusion of small zoos in public parks reflected the awakening appeal of animals.

The development of recreation grounds

Initially, those responsible for the development of early municipal parks perceived 'sporting activities' as an anti-social activity of the working classes. The 1833 Select Committee on Public Walks saw walking as the primary recreation. It was not until the late nineteenth century that municipal parks were boasting bowling greens, tennis courts and gymnasiums (*Elliot and Fieldhouse*[12]).

In the early twentieth century, small recreation grounds began to appear that were designed specifically for games. The physical fitness of the male population had been a concern of successive governments from the time of the Boer War (1899-1902) (*Harrison*). In an attempt to ensure that the next generation of soldiers were fit to fight, early attempts to develop and justify recreation provision were made according to a set of 'Open Space Standards' developed by the National Playing Fields Association. Since 1938, local authorities have used the 'Six Acre Standard' to calculate recreation and children's play area provision. The standard is based on an estimate of the numbers of youth and adults who would like to participate in team sports such as football and cricket (*Harrison*).

Countryside recreation

'In Victorian Society, educated people have regarded the countryside as a place for dreams and yearnings

6

– a golden age that represented all that the city was not.' (cited in *Harrison*[3])

In the nineteenth century, the vociferous defence of urban commons and public open space was prompted by the enclosures. Between 1836 and 1845, following public pressure and the recommendation of a Select Committee, the government intervened to protect common land through General Inclosure Acts (*Harrison*).

Between 1850 and 1860, for those with newly-found wealth, the countryside became a place for sport and weekend resort. Country sports such as fox hunting, deer stalking, grouse and pheasant shooting flourished. The growing passion for country sport was legitimised by the Game Act 1831, which permitted the sale of shooting and hunting permits on private estates (*Harrison*).

By 1900, transport improvements and changes in people's mobility meant that the countryside was easily accessible to those living in the urban environment. The demand for recreation moved away from urban parks and open spaces to the countryside. This generated conflict between landowners and the general public. By the 1930s, during the depression, the continued erosion of public rights of way resulted in mass trespasses as people turned to the countryside for cheap holidays and day excursions (*Harrison*). The Forestry Commission took very positive steps to harmonise its relationship with the public and allowed low-key recreational activity to take place within its sites. The move was popular and, in 1949, access to the countryside was established within National Parks legislation.

Watering places and spa resorts

The seaside holiday originated in Scarborough. From as early as 1626, Scarborough's fame was forged by the discovery of a spring, which ran from the cliffs on to the beach. A local entrepreneur quickly exploited the spring's medicinal properties and, by 1667, the medical profession had endorsed the health-giving properties of spas, creating an era that was to last 150 years.

Britain's mercantile empire had created a new rich class of shippers, entrepreneurs, traders and bankers who were affluent enough to have leisure time. One of the ways this was spent was the taking of the 'cure'. High society travelled far and wide in search of spiritual or physical medication. The city of Bath was rediscovered and, together with Buxton and Harrogate, flourished as a spa town.

Scarborough's spa was in direct competition with those in Buxton and Harrogate. In a bid for greater attention, Scarborough made a claim that was to surpass all inland spas: the sea was promoted. Bathing and drinking salt water ran together as seaside resorts quickly grew in size and number. This gave rise to the name 'watering places'.

Early in the history of the seaside, resorts were exclusive to the upper classes. High fashion took to the waters. It was suggested that the popularity of watering places, for the upper classes, owed something to the over-popularity of the inland spas for the new wave of middle class. By the late eighteenth century and early nineteenth century, the people who frequented the coast expected the same facilities found at inland spas, such as assembly rooms, libraries, theatres and promenades.

Towards the middle of the nineteenth century, drinking seawater became less important than doing the social round. In the end, fashion and science turned against the drinking of seawater. By 1850, the mineral water habit had arrived from the continent. Brighton became the first resort proper to shed its reputation as a watering place.

Spas and seaside resorts coarsened over the subsequent years as the aristocracy moved on to the spas of Germany. The railways opened the coast to town dwellers and these took advantage of the opportunity to have a good time. The Bank Holiday Act 1871 gave an impetus to the social habit of 'tripping to the seaside' (*Hern*). A latent demand for day excursions was realised. Each year, in Queen Victoria's reign, day trips and holidays to the seaside increased. It has been suggested that part of the boom of the seaside in Victorian times was due to the increasing unpleasantness of the home environment (*Hern*).

In the period between the wars, as more workers received holiday pay, resorts competed among themselves for custom by creating amenities. Blackpool spent £1,500,000 on creating the seven-mile promenade and £250,000 laying out a park (*Hern*). In a little over 150 years, the English holiday had become an industry with an incredible investment to match.

The 'appeal to health' (*Hern*) had a negative affect on the popularity of some resorts. As medicine advanced, so illnesses became less lingering. Initially, watering places had been established to make money from the middle-class invalid so those resorts that had developed an infrastructure to cater for such a person found trade dropping off.

Early legislation of minor importance
Early national legislation for parks and open spaces, in the mid-nineteenth century, signified a growing public awareness of the need to provide pleasant places where

people could have free access. Many of our earlier parks were provided under such legislation or through local Acts of Parliament. Although such powers are rarely used to acquire or manage parks and open space in modern times, managers need to have awareness of the powers under which their parks, open spaces and associated facilities were provided. Unless local legislation has been repealed, such early legislation may still have a significant affect on the management and control of such land. With the exception of local legislation, the earlier Acts of relevance are:

1. The Recreation Grounds Act 1859.

2. The Town Gardens Protection Act 1863.

3. The Public Improvements Act 1860.

The Recreation Grounds Act 1859

The Recreation Grounds Act 1859 empowered charities to provide open public lands for use as playgrounds (suitable for children and the youth) and land for adult recreation. Although the 1859 Act was repealed in full by the Charities Act 1960, a number of trusts of charity are still wholly comprised under the 1859 Act or within an instrument having effect under the Act. The operation of those trusts is not affected by the repeal. Consequently, although the 1859 Act was repealed in full, it is still relevant for some charities. Most of the earlier properties owned by the National Playing Fields Association are vested to them under the provisions of the 1859 Act.

The Town Gardens Protection Act 1863

The Town Gardens Protection Act 1863 empowers local authorities, in cities and towns, to take charge of enclosed gardens or ornamental grounds and either establish a management committee or maintain the grounds themselves. Management committees are able to make byelaws for the preservation of a garden or ground within this statute.

The Public Improvements Act 1860
The Public Improvements Act 1860 was repealed by the Parish Councils Act 1957. It provided discretionary powers to any borough or parish council with a population of five hundred or more to purchase, lease or accept a gift of land for the purpose of forming public walks, playgrounds and allowing exercise. It subsequently provided powers to levy a rate for maintenance and control of sites. Prior to being allowed to levy a rate, the Act had one major disadvantage in that 50% of the estimated cost of any proposed improvement would have to be raised, given or collected by private subscription or donation.

Early legislation of significant importance
In the late nineteenth century, local legislation continued to have a significant role in the provision of parks and open spaces, and was often used to overcome local difficulties or provide wider powers than were available within legislation at the time. Three significant pieces of legislation in the development of parks and open spaces, and of relevance to the modern day manager, are:

1. The Public Health Act 1875.

2. The Open Spaces Act 1906.

3. The Physical Training and Recreation Act 1937.

The Public Health Act 1875
Section 164 of the Public Health Act 1875 gave local authorities specific discretionary powers to provide and maintain public walks and pleasure grounds.

The provisions within the 1875 Act consisted of two paragraphs:

> 'Any [urban] authority may purchase or take on lease lay out plant improve and maintain lands for the purpose of being used as public walks or pleasure grounds and may support or contribute to the support of public walks or pleasure grounds provided by any person whomsoever.'

> 'Any [urban] authority may make a byelaw for the regulation of any such public walk or pleasure ground, and may by such byelaws provide for the removal from such public walk or pleasure ground of any person infringing any such byelaw by any officer of the [urban] authority or constable.'

By virtue of paragraph 27 of Schedule 14 to the Local Government Act 1972, the 1875 Act is now appropriate to all local authorities:

(1) The powers conferred on certain authorities by the enactments to which this paragraph applies shall be exercised not only by those authorities, but also by all local authorities within the meaning of this Act, whether or not they are local authorities for the purposes of the Public Health Acts 1875 to 1925, and references in those enactments to an urban authority or a local authority shall be construed accordingly.

(2) This paragraph applies to the following enactments, that is to say—

   (a) Section 164 of the Public Health Act 1875

   ...

The Open Spaces Act 1906
The Open Spaces Act 1906 gave powers to trustees under local Acts of Parliament to transfer open spaces, recreation grounds and disused burial grounds to local authorities. Local authorities were given power to acquire by agreement open spaces and disused burial grounds and to manage such areas for public benefit. An open space was defined to include not only land used for recreation but also land laid out as a garden or which was waste and unoccupied.

The Physical Training and Recreation Act 1937
The Physical Training and Recreation Act 1937 did not make the 1875 Act obsolete. It moved provision away from the Victorian idea of 'public walk' and 'pleasure grounds' to 'playing fields, gymnasiums, swimming baths, bathing places, holiday camps, camping sites, and other buildings and premises for physical training'. The Act provides strong links with the world of education. The 1937 Act was passed as a result of the 'keep-fit' campaign, a 'new movement for the improvement of national physique'.

ENDNOTES

1 Briggs, ASA, *A Social History of England*, 2nd Edition, 1994, The Orion Publishing Group.

2 Strong, R, *The Story of Britain*, 1998, Pimlico.

3 Harrison, C, *Countryside Recreation in a Changing Society*, 1st edition, 1991, The TMS Partnership Ltd.

4 Rubinstein, WD, *Britain's Century – A Political and Social History 1815-1905*, 1st Edition, 1998, Arnold.

5 Hern, A, *The Seaside Holiday*, 1967, Cresset Press.

6 Gill, C, *History of Birmingham*, Vol 1, 1952, Oxford University Press, cited in Stewart, J, *The Nature of British Local Government*, 1st Edition, 2000, Macmillan.

7 Conway, H and Lambert, D, *Public Prospects: Historic Urban Parks Under Threat*, 1993, Garden History Society and Victorian Society.

8 Rodger, Dr R, 'Controlling The Built Environment' in *Urbanisation in Britain 1780–1914*, CD, 2005, History Courseware Consortium.

9 Select Committee on Public Works, BPP, Vol XV (1833), Cmnd. 448, cited in Woudstra, J and Fieldhouse, K, *The Regeneration of Public Parks*, 1st Edition, 2000, E & FN Spon.

10 Beresford, M, *History on the Ground*, 1998, Sutton Publishing.

11 Commission's Inquiry (Second Report) into the state of large towns and populations, 1844.

12 Elliot, B and Fieldhouse, K, *Play and Sport*, cited in Woudstra, J and Fieldhouse, K, *The Regeneration of Public Parks*, 1st Edition, 2000, E & FN Spon.

Chapter 2

ACQUISITION OF PARKS AND OPEN SPACES

Acquisition of land by agreement or gift

Introduction

The powers of local authorities to acquire land by agreement or gift are largely contained in the Local Government Act 1972 (LGA 1972). The legislation makes separate provision for principal councils and for local councils. The Open Spaces Act 1906 also gives local authorities powers to acquire land (see page 19 below).

Acquisition of land by agreement or gift by principal councils

Section 120 of the LGA 1972 states as follows:

(1) For the purposes of—

    (a) any of their functions under this or any other enactment, or

    (b) the benefit, improvement or development of their area,

a principal council may acquire by agreement any land, whether situated inside or outside their area.

(2) A principal council may acquire by agreement any land for any purpose for which they are authorised by this or any other enactment to acquire land, notwithstanding that the land is not immediately required for that purpose; and, until it is required for the purpose for which it was acquired, any land acquired under this subsection may be used for the purpose of any of the council's functions.

15

(3) Where under this section a council are authorised to acquire land by agreement, the provisions of Part I of the Compulsory Purchase Act 1965 (so far as applicable) other than section 31 shall apply, and in the said Part I as so applied the word 'land' shall have the meaning assigned to it by this Act.

(4) Where two or more councils acting together would have power to acquire any land by agreement by virtue of this section, nothing in any enactment shall prevent one of those councils from so acquiring the land on behalf of both or all of them in accordance with arrangements made between them, including arrangements as to the subsequent occupation and use of the land.

(5) References in the foregoing provisions of this section to acquisition by agreement are references to acquisition for money or money's worth, as purchaser or lessee.

Subsection (3) is important in that it allows principal authorities to override restrictive covenants on the acquisition of land by agreement, as well as by compulsory purchase.

Subsection (4) provides that section 120 does not apply to an acquisition by gift. Section 139 of the LGA 1972 authorises a local authority to accept a gift of real or personal property for the purpose of discharging a statutory function or for the benefit of the inhabitants of their area or part of it. However, there is no power to accept a gift of property for the purposes of an ecclesiastical charity or a charity for the relief of poverty.

Acquisition of land by agreement or gift by a local council
Section 124 of the LGA 1972 gives local councils the same powers of land acquisition by agreement as principal

councils, save that local councils do not have the power to acquire land in advance of need as set out in section 120(2) of the Act.

Local councils also have the same powers as principal councils to accept gifts of real or personal property.

Acquisition of land compulsorily

If a council is unable to acquire land by agreement, it has statutory powers to acquire that land compulsorily for one or more of its statutory functions, unless the power of acquisition is specifically restricted to acquisition by agreement.

Acquisition of land compulsorily by principal councils

Section 121 of the LGA 1972 deals with this matter and is set out below:

121.—(1) Subject to subsection (2) below, for any purpose for which they are authorised by this or any other public general Act to acquire land, a principal council may be authorised by the Minister concerned with that purpose to purchase compulsorily any land, whether situated inside or outside their area.

(2) A council may not be authorised under subsection (1) above to purchase land compulsorily—

(a) for the purpose specified in section 120(1)(b) above, or

(b) for the purpose of any of their functions under the Local Authorities (Land) Act 1963, or

(c) for any purpose in relation to which their power of acquisition is by any enactment

> expressly limited to acquisition by agreement.

(3) Where one or more councils propose, in exercise of the power conferred by subsection (1) above, to acquire any land for more than one purpose, the Minister or Ministers whose authorisation is required for the exercise of that power shall not be concerned to make any apportionment between those purposes nor, where there is more than one council, between those councils, and—

> (a) the purposes shall be treated as a single purpose and the compulsory acquisition shall be treated as requiring the authorisation of the Minister, or the joint authorisation of the Ministers, concerned with those purposes; and

> (b) where there is more than one council concerned, the councils may nominate one of them to acquire the land on behalf of them all and the council so nominated shall accordingly be treated as the acquiring authority for the purposes of any enactment relating to the acquisition.

(4) The Acquisition of Land Act 1981 shall apply in relation to the compulsory purchase of land in pursuance of subsection (1) above.

The limitations are as follows. First, they may not use the section for the acquisition of land for 'the benefit, improvement or development of their area'. They may do this by agreement as explained above. Secondly, they may not use the section for the purpose of any of their functions under the Local Authorities (Land) Act 1963. Thirdly, they may not exercise compulsory powers for any purpose in relation to which their power of acquisition is by any enactment expressly limited to acquisition by agreement, as in the case of the power to purchase land for use as an open space or burial ground under section 9 of the Open Spaces Act 1906.

Acquisition of land compulsorily on behalf of local councils
Here the provisions of section 125 of the LGA 1972 are complicated because district councils have the power to buy compulsorily on behalf of local councils. Note the somewhat tedious procedural requirements involved in the section which reads as follows:

125.—(1) If a parish or community council are unable to acquire by agreement under section 124 above and on reasonable terms suitable land for any purpose for which they are authorised to acquire land other than—

(a) the purpose specified in section 124(1)(b) above, or

(b) any purpose in relation to which the power of acquisition is by any enactment expressly limited to acquisition by agreement,

they may represent the case to the council of the district in which the parish or community is situated.

(2) If the district council are satisfied that suitable land for the purpose cannot be acquired on reasonable terms by agreement, they may be authorised by the Secretary of State to purchase compulsorily

the land or part of it; and the Acquisition of Land Act 1981 shall apply in relation to the purchase.

(3) The district council in making and the Secretary of State in confirming an order for the purposes of this section shall have regard to the extent of land held in the neighbourhood by an owner and to the convenience of other property belonging to the same owner and shall, as far as practicable, avoid taking an undue or inconvenient quantity of land from any one owner.

(4) The order shall be carried into effect by the district council but the land when acquired shall be conveyed to the parish or community council; and accordingly in construing for the purposes of this section and of the order any enactment applying in relation to the compulsory acquisition, the parish or community council or the district council, or the two councils jointly, shall, as case may require, be treated as the acquiring authority.

(5) The district council may recover from the parish or community council the expenses incurred by them in connection with the acquisition of land under this section.

(6) If a parish or community council make representations to a district council with a view to the making of an order under this section and the district council—

(a) refuse to make an order, or

(b) do not make an order within 8 weeks from the making of the representations or such longer period as may be agreed between the two councils,

the parish or community council may petition the Secretary of State who may make the order, and this section and the provisions of the Acquisition of Land Act 1981 shall apply as if the order had been made by the district council and confirmed by the Secretary of State.

(7) In the application of this section to a parish or community council for a group of parishes or communities—

(a) references to the parish or community shall be construed as references to the area of the group, and

(b) if different parts of the area of the group lie in different districts, references to the council of the district in which the parish or community is situated shall be construed as references to the councils of each of the districts acting jointly.

(8) In relation to Wales—

(a) references in this section to a district council are to be read as references to a principal council; and

(b) references to a district are to be read as references to a principal area.

Appropriation of land

Local authorities have statutory powers to appropriate land from use for one statutory function to another.

Appropriation of land by principal councils

The main legislation allowing principal councils to appropriate land from use for one statutory purpose to another is contained in section 122 of the LGA 1972. The section is as follows:

> 122.—(1) Subject to the following provisions of this section, a principal council may appropriate for any purpose for which the council are authorised by this or any other enactment to acquire land by agreement any land which belongs to the council and is no longer required for the purpose for which it is held immediately before the appropriation; but the appropriation of land by a council by virtue of this subsection shall be subject to the rights of other persons in, over or in respect of the land concerned.
>
> (2) A principal council may not appropriate under subsection (1) above any land which they may be authorised to appropriate under section 229 of the Town and Country Planning Act 1990 (land forming part of a common etc), unless—
>
> > (a) the total of the land appropriated in any particular common, or fuel or field garden allotment (giving those expressions the same meanings as in the said section 229) does not in the aggregate exceed 250 square yards, and
> >
> > (b) before appropriating the land they cause notice of their intention to do so, specifying the land in question, to be advertised in two consecutive weeks in a newspaper circulating in the area in which the land is

situated, and consider any objections to the proposed appropriation which may be made to them.

(2A) A principal council may not appropriate under subsection (1) above any land consisting or forming part of an open space unless before appropriating the land they cause notice of their intention to do so, specifying the land in question, to be advertised in two consecutive weeks in a newspaper circulating in the area in which the land is situated, and consider any objections to the proposed appropriation which may be made to them.

(2B) Where land appropriated by virtue of subsection (2A) above is held—

(a) for the purposes of section 164 of the Public Health Act 1875 (pleasure grounds), or

(b) in accordance with section 10 of the Open Spaces Act 1906 (duty of local authority to maintain open spaces and burial grounds),

the land shall by virtue of the appropriation be freed from any trust arising solely by virtue of its being land held in trust for enjoyment by the public in accordance with the said section 164 or, as the case may be, the said section 10.

[(3) repealed by the Local Government and Planning Act 1980.]

(4) Where land has been acquired under this Act or any other enactment or any statutory order incorporating the Lands Clauses Acts and is

subsequently appropriated under this section, any work executed on the land after the appropriation has been effected shall be treated for the purposes of section 68 of the Lands Clauses Consolidation Act 1845 and section 10 of the Compulsory Purchase Act 1965 as having been authorised by the enactment or statutory order under which the land was acquired.

Section 229 of the Town and Country Planning Act 1990 (TCPA 1990) provides as follows:

229.—(1) Any local authority may be authorised, by an order made by that authority and confirmed by the Secretary of State, to appropriate for any purpose for which that authority can be authorised to acquire land under any enactment any land for the time being held by them for other purposes.

(2) Subsection (1) applies to land which is or forms part of a common, or fuel or field garden allotment (including any such land which is specially regulated by any enactment, whether public general or local or private), other than land which is Green Belt land within the meaning of the Green Belt (London and Home Counties) Act 1938.

(3) Section 19 of the Acquisition of Land Act 1981 (special provisions with respect to compulsory purchase orders under that Act relating to land forming part of a common, open space or fuel or field garden allotment) shall apply to an order under this section authorising the appropriation of land as it applies to a compulsory purchase order under that Act.

(4) Where land appropriated under this section was acquired under an enactment incorporating the Lands Clauses Acts, any works executed on the land after the appropriation has been effected shall, for the purposes of section 68 of the Lands Clauses Consolidation Act 1845 and section 10 of the Compulsory Purchase Act 1965 be deemed to have been authorised by the enactment under which the land was acquired.

'Common' and 'open space' are defined in section 336 of the TCPA 1990 thus:

'common' includes any land subject to be enclosed under the Inclosure Acts 1845 to 1882 and any town or village green;

'open space' means any land laid out as a public garden, or used for the purposes of public recreation, or land which is a disused burial ground.

Section 19 of the Acquisition of Land Act 1981 applies to an order made under section 229 of the TCPA 1990 and is as follows:

19.—(1) In so far as a compulsory purchase order authorises the purchase of any land forming part of a common, open space or fuel or field garden allotment, the order shall be subject to special parliamentary procedure unless the Secretary of State is satisfied—

(a) that there has been or will be given in exchange for such land, other land, not being less in area and being equally advantageous to the persons, if any, entitled to rights of common or other rights, and to the public, and that the land given in exchange has been or will be vested in the persons in whom the land purchased was vested, and subject to the like rights, trusts and incidents as attach to the land purchased, or

(aa) the land is being purchased in order to secure its preservation or improve its management,

(b) that the land does not exceed 250 square yards in extent or is required for the widening or drainage of an existing highway or partly for the widening and partly for the drainage of such a highway and that the giving in exchange of other land is unnecessary, whether in the interests of the persons, if any, entitled to rights of common or other rights or in the interests of the public, and certifies accordingly.

(2) Where it is proposed to give a certificate under this section, the Secretary of State shall direct the acquiring authority to give public notice of his intention to do so, and—

(a) after affording opportunity to all persons interested to make representations and objections in relation thereto, and

(b) after causing a public local inquiry to be held in any case where it appears to him to be expedient so to do, having regard to any representations or objections made,

the Secretary of State may, after considering any representations and objections made and, if an inquiry has been held, the report of the person who held the inquiry, give the certificate.

(2A) Notice under subsection (2) above shall be given in such form and manner as the Secretary of State may direct.

(3) A compulsory purchase order may provide for—

(a) vesting land given in exchange as mentioned in subsection (1) above in the persons, and subject to the rights, trusts and incidents, therein mentioned, and

(b) discharging the land purchased from all rights, trusts and incidents to which it was previously subject except where the Secretary of State has given a certificate under subsection (1)(aa) above.

(4) In this section—

'common' includes any land subject to be enclosed under the Inclosure Acts 1845 to 1882, and any town or village green;

'fuel or field garden allotment' means any allotment set out as a fuel allotment, or a field garden allotment, under an Inclosure Act;

'open space' means any land laid out as a public garden, or used for the purposes of public recreation, or land being a disused burial ground.

Appropriation of land by local councils

Section 126 of the LGA 1972 enables a local council to appropriate land from one purpose to another. In a parish where there is no council, the parish meeting may appropriate land with the consent of the Secretary of State. A community meeting in Wales has no power of appropriation. The section is as follows:

> 126.—(1) Any land belonging to a parish or community council which is not required for the purposes for which it was acquired or has since been appropriated may, subject to the following provisions of this section, be appropriated by the council for any other purpose for which the council are authorised by this or any other public general Act to acquire land by agreement.
>
> (2) In the case of a parish which does not have a separate parish council, any land belonging to the parish meeting which is not required for the purposes for which it was acquired or has since been appropriated may, subject to the following provisions of this section, be appropriated by the parish meeting for any other purpose approved by the Secretary of State.
>
> (3) The appropriation of land by virtue of this section by a parish or community council or by a parish meeting shall be subject to the rights of other persons in, over or in respect of the land concerned.
>
> (4) Neither a parish or community council nor a parish meeting may appropriate by virtue of this section any land which they may be authorised to appropriate under section 229 of the Town and Country Planning Act 1990 (land forming part of a common, etc) unless—
>
>> (a) the total of the land appropriated in any particular common, or fuel or field garden

allotment (giving those expressions the same meanings as in the said section 229) does not in the aggregate exceed 250 square yards, and

(b) before appropriating the land they cause notice of their intention to do so, specifying the land in question, to be advertised in two consecutive weeks in a newspaper circulating in the area in which the land is situated, and consider any objections to the proposed appropriation which may be made to them.

Planning obligations

Sections 106, 106A and 106B of the TCPA 1990 relate to planning obligations. Section 106 enables a planning obligation to be entered into by means of a unilateral undertaking by a landowner or by agreement between a landowner and a local planning authority.

Section 106(1) provides that anyone with an interest in land may enter into a planning obligation enforceable by the local planning authority identified in the instrument creating the obligation. Such an obligation may be created by agreement or by the person with the interest making an undertaking and may:

(a) restrict development or use of the land;

(b) require operations or activities to be carried out in, on, under or over the land;

(c) require the land to be used in any specified way; or

(d) require payments to be made to the authority either in a single sum or periodically.

The obligations created run with the land and may be enforced against both the original covenantor and against anyone acquiring an interest in the land from him unless the agreement makes specific to the contrary.

Section 106(2) provides that a planning obligation may:

(a) be unconditional or subject to conditions;

(b) impose any restriction or requirement in 106(1)(a) to (c) for an indefinite or specified period;

(c) provide for payments of money to be made, either of a specific amount or by reference to a formula, and require periodical payments to be paid indefinitely or for a specified period.

Section 106(3) provides that planning obligations are enforceable against the original covenantor and his successors in title.

Section 106(4) enables the instrument which creates the planning obligation to limit the liability of covenantors to the period before they cease to have an interest in the land.

Section 106(5) provides for restrictions or requirements imposed under a planning obligation to be enforced by injunction.

Section 106(6) provides that, in addition to section 106(5), if there is a breach of a requirement to carry out works on the land, the authority may enter the land and carry out the works itself and recover its reasonable expenses.

Section 106(7) provides that the authority, before exercising its powers to enter the land, shall give not less than 21 days' notice of its intention to do so to any person against whom the obligation is enforceable.

Section 106(8) provides that any person who wilfully obstructs the authority if it enters the land under subsection (6)(a) is guilty of an offence and is liable to a maximum fine of level 3 on the standard scale (currently £1,000).

Section 106(9) requires that a planning obligation may only be entered into by a deed which:

(a) states that the obligation created is a planning obligation;

(b) identifies the land concerned;

(c) identifies the person entering into the obligation and states his interest; and

(d) identifies the authority by whom the obligation may be enforced.

Section 106(10) requires a copy of the deed to be given to the local planning authority by whom it is enforceable.

Section 106(11) provides that a planning obligation is a local land charge for the purposes of the Local Land Charges Act 1975. If a local land charge is not registered, it remains binding against a purchaser of the land, but the purchaser is entitled to compensation for non-registration. Under section 8 of the 1975 Act, any member of the public has a right of access to the local land charges register, which is maintained by every London borough and district council. The register contains a description of the charge, including a reference to the relevant statutory provision, and says where relevant documents may be inspected.

Section 106(12) enables the Secretary of State to make regulations specifying that money to be paid, or expenses recoverable, under a planning obligation is a charge on the land.

Section 106(13) defines the terms 'land' and 'specified' used in section 106.

Section 106A(1) provides that a planning obligation may not be modified or discharged except by agreement between the authority and the person or persons against whom it is enforceable, or in accordance with sections 106A(1) and 106B.

Section 106A(2) provides that any agreement between the parties to modify or discharge a planning obligation shall be by deed.

Section 106A(3) provides that anyone against whom a planning obligation is enforceable may, at any time after the 'relevant period' expires, apply to the local planning authority concerned for the obligation to be modified as specified in his/her application or for it to be discharged.

Section 106A(4) defines 'relevant period' as such period as may be prescribed by the Secretary of State in regulations, failing which the period is to be five years from the date the obligation is entered into.

Section 106A(5) prevents any applicant for modification of a planning obligation from specifying a modification which imposes an obligation on some other person against whom the original obligation is enforceable.

Section 106A(6) provides that an authority which receives an application for modification or discharge of a planning obligation may determine it by refusing it; or, if the obligation no longer serves any useful purpose, by discharging it; or, if the obligation would serve a useful purpose equally well with the modifications specified by the applicant, by consenting to the modifications sought.

Section 106A(7) provides that the authority shall notify the applicant of its decision within a period prescribed by the Secretary of State.

Section 106A(8) provides that, where the authority determines that a planning obligation has effect subject to modification, the modified obligation is enforceable from the date on which the applicant is sent a notice of determination.

Section 106A(9) empowers the Secretary of State to make regulations with respect to the form and content of applications, the publication of notices of such applications, procedures for considering any representations on the applications and the notices to be given to applicants of the authority's determination.

Section 106A(10) provides that section 84 of the Law of Property Act 1925 does not apply to planning obligations. Section 84 empowers the Lands Tribunal to modify or discharge restrictive covenants, including those contained in a planning obligation.

Section 106B(1) provides that, where a local planning authority fails to give notice of its determination of an application for modification or discharge of a planning obligation within the period prescribed under section 106A(7), or to refuse such an application (see section 106A(6)(a)), the applicant may appeal to the Secretary of State.

Section 106B(2) provides that an appeal against an authority's failure to give notice of its determination of an application is treated in the same way as an appeal against refusal of an application.

Section 106B(3) enables the Secretary of State to make

regulations prescribing the period within which notice of such appeals are given and the manner in which they are made.

Section 106B(4) applies 106A(6) to (9) in relation to appeals to the Secretary of State as they apply in relation to applications to authorities.

Section 106B(5) gives either party to an appeal the right to a hearing.

Section 106B(6) provides that the determination of an appeal to the Secretary of State under this section is final.

Section 106B(7) applies Schedule 6 to the 1990 Act (Determination of Certain Appeals by Person Appointed by Secretary of State), allowing appeals to be determined by an inspector appointed by the Secretary of State. The procedure is governed by the Town and Country Planning (Modification and Discharge of Planning Obligations) Regulations 1992 (SI 1992/2832) (as amended).

The Department for Communities and Local Government (DCLG) has issued a circular on planning obligations entitled *Circular 05/2005: Planning Obligations.* This can be viewed on the DCLG website at www. communities.gov.uk/publications/planningandbuilding/ circularplanningobligations. The equivalent Welsh publication is Welsh Office Circular 13/97 *Planning Obligations.*

Sections 106, 106A and 106B are prospectively repealed by section 118 of and Schedule 6 to the Planning and Compulsory Purchase Act 2004. At the time of writing, no date for repeal had been set.

Local Acts of Parliament

Many local authorities acquired land for public parks under powers obtained in local Acts of Parliament. By virtue of section 262(9) of the LGA 1972, all such local Acts and other local statutory provisions expired in metropolitan counties at the end of 1979 and elsewhere at the end of 1984, unless the Secretary of State made an order postponing the termination date or exempting a local statutory provision from the provisions of the subsection.

Some local authorities have obtained new local Acts re-enacting provisions which would have expired under the section 262(9).

Chapter 3

DISPOSAL OF PARKS AND OPEN SPACES

Disposal of land by principal councils

Section 123 of the LGA 1972 provides for the disposal of land by principal authorities and is as follows:

> 123.—(1) Subject to the following provisions of this section, a principal council may dispose of land held by them in any manner they wish.
>
> (2) Except with the consent of the Secretary of State, a council shall not dispose of land under this section, otherwise than by way of a short tenancy, for a consideration less than the best that can reasonably be obtained.
>
> (2A) A principal council may not dispose under subsection (1) above of any land consisting or forming part of an open space unless before disposing of the land they cause notice of their intention to do so, specifying the land in question, to be advertised in two consecutive weeks in a newspaper circulating in the area in which the land is situated, and consider any objections to the proposed disposal which may be made to them.
>
> (2B) Where by virtue of subsection (2A) above a council dispose of land which is held—
>
> (a) for the purposes of section 164 of the Public Health Act 1875 (pleasure grounds); or

37

(b) in accordance with section 10 of the Open Spaces Act 1906 (duty of local authority to maintain open spaces and burial grounds),

the land shall by virtue of the disposal be freed from any trust arising solely by virtue of its being land held in trust for enjoyment by the public in accordance with the said section 164 or, as the case may be, the said section 10.

[Subsections (3) to (6) repealed]

(7) For the purposes of this section a disposal of land is a disposal by way of a short tenancy if it consists—

(a) of a grant of a term not exceeding seven years, or

(b) of the assignment of a term which at the date of the assignment has not more than seven years to run,

and in this section 'public trust land' has the meaning assigned to it by section 122(6) above. (Section 122(6) was repealed by the Local Government, Planning and Land Act 1980.)

Under section 123 of the LGA 1972, the disposal of common land or town or village greens by agreement is not subject to the Secretary of State's approval if it is sold for not less than the best consideration reasonably obtainable. However, the land retains the status as common or green and the new owner has to consider his own powers to obtain an alternative use, for instance by way of compulsory purchase or exchange.

Disposal of land by local councils

Local councils have the same powers and are subject to the same limitations as apply to principal councils. The relevant section is as follows:

127.—(1) Subject to the following provisions of this section, a parish or community council, or the parish trustees of a parish acting with the consent of the parish meeting, may dispose of land held by them in any manner they wish.

(2) Except with the consent of the Secretary of State, land shall not be disposed of under this section, otherwise than by way of a short tenancy, for a consideration other than the best that can reasonably be obtained.

(3) Subsections (2A) and (2B) of section 123 above shall apply in relation to the disposal of land under this section as they apply to the disposal of land under that section, with the substitution of a reference to a parish or community council or the parish trustees of a parish meeting for the reference to a principal council in the said subsection (2A).

(4) Capital money received in respect of a disposal under this section of land held for charitable purposes shall be applied in accordance with any directions given under the Charities Act 1993.

(5) For the purposes of this section a disposal of land is a disposal by way of a short tenancy if it consists—

(a) of the grant of a tenancy not exceeding seven years, or

(b) of the assignment of a tenancy which at the date of the assignment has not more than seven years to run.

Consents to land transactions by local authorities and protection of purchasers

Section 128 of the LGA 1972 gives the Secretary of State wide powers to dispense with the need to obtain consent to dealings in land and to attach conditions to consents. A purchaser is not concerned to see that any of the statutory requirements as to consent or other requirements have been met.

The predecessor of the Department for Communities and Local Government (the Office of the Deputy Prime Minister) issued a circular on the disposal of land by local authorities in England in August 2003, entitled *Circular 06/03: Local Government Act 1972. General disposal consent (England). Consent for the disposal of land for less than the best consideration that can reasonably be obtained*. The circular can be viewed on the Department's website at: www.communities.gov.uk/publications/planningandbuilding/circularlocalgovernment.

In Wales, the Assembly issued a similar circular in December 2003. This can be viewed on the Assembly's local government website at: http://new.wales.gov.uk/publications/circular/circulars03/NAFWC412003?lang=en.

Land held subject to trusts, covenants and agreements
General

By section 131(1)(a) of the 1972 Act, the disposal of any land is made subject to compliance with restrictions, excluding any trust arising solely by reason of the land being held as public walks and pleasure grounds or in accordance with section 10 of the Open Spaces Act 1906.

Provisions in local Acts dealing with, *inter alia*, lands the subject of this book, have to be complied with notwithstanding the foregoing provisions of this Part of the LGA 1972 dealing with transactions in land, etc. Similarly, nothing therein contained is to affect the operation of section 36 of the Charities Act 1993 (restrictions on dispositions of charity land).

Generally speaking, the disposal of land subject to charitable trusts must be for the best consideration reasonably obtainable, subject to the detailed provisions of Part V of the Charities Act 1993.

Fuel allotment charities created by inclosure awards
These are charitable trust lands which were created when rights of common were extinguished by inclosure. Generally, the land was to be held in trust for one of two purposes:

(a) to provide fuel – either furze or turf – in kind;

(b) to provide rents with which to buy fuel or other benefits.

Schedule 4 to the Charities Act 1993 provides that, notwithstanding anything in section 19 of the Commons Act 1876 (which made it unlawful to divert fuel allotments to other uses), a scheme for the administration of a fuel allotment (within the meaning of the foregoing paragraph) may provide:

(a) for the sale or letting of the allotment or any part thereof, for the discharge of the land sold or let from any restrictions as to the use thereof imposed by or under any enactment relating to inclosure and for the application of the sums payable to the trustees of the allotment in respect of the sale or lease; or

41

(b) for the exchange of the allotment or any part thereof for other land, for the discharge as aforesaid of the land given in exchange by the trustees, and for the application of any money payable to the trustees for equality of exchange; or

(c) for the use of the allotment or any part thereof for any purposes specified in the scheme.

Other charitable property
Section 139 of the LGA 1972 empowers local authorities (but not parish meetings) to accept, hold and administer any gifts of land made for the benefit of the inhabitants of their area or of some part of it or for the purpose of discharging any of their statutory functions.

The Charity Commission's publication *Charities and Local Authorities* (CC 29) gives detailed guidance on the involvement of local authorities in the running of charities.

Chapter 4

PROVISION AND MANAGEMENT OF PARKS AND OPEN SPACES

Statutory powers of management

The earliest statute still in force giving powers of management of open spaces is the Town Gardens Protection Act 1863. Under this Act, gardens or ornamental grounds set aside for the use and enjoyment of the inhabitants of a city or borough may be protected by corporate bodies of such places, who may, in certain circumstances, take charge of those areas. Where the owners or occupiers of houses and other property having the benefit of such land do not agree to undertake charge of it, the protection authority must vest the land in the local authority.

Byelaws may be made by the committee of management of inhabitants. Byelaws may also be made by a local authority under the Open Spaces Act 1906 – see below and Chapter 5 on byelaws.

The boroughs existing immediately before 1st April 1974 were abolished on that date by the Local Government Act 1972, so that the reference to a borough in the 1863 Act no longer has any effect. County boroughs in Wales established by the Local Government Act 1994 are not to be treated as boroughs for the purposes of any Act passed before 1st April 1974 (section 64(2) of the 1994 Act). As a result, the only local authorities to which the 1863 Act applies are London borough councils and the Common Council of the City of London.

The 1972 Act did not in terms abolish cities which existed immediately before 1st April 1974. However, outside

Greater London, a city was not a distinct and separate type of local authority, so that the abolition of all local authorities, except rural parishes (renamed parishes), by the 1972 Act effectively abolished any city authorities other than those which were parishes. Presumably, therefore, the 1863 Act applies to any parishes with the status of city, at least where that status was acquired before 1st April 1974. The 1863 Act does not apply to those local authorities granted city status under the Local Government Act 2000.

Public walks and pleasure grounds

Under section 164 of the Public Health Act 1875, any 'urban authority' may purchase or take on lease, lay out, plant, improve and maintain lands for the purpose of being used as public walks or pleasure grounds, and may support or contribute to the support of public walks or pleasure grounds provided by any other person. The authority may make byelaws for the regulation of such public grounds. The byelaws may provide for the removal of any person infringing a byelaw by any officer of the urban authority or by a constable.

The powers to acquire, lay out, etc. were extended by sections 44 and 45 of the Public Health Acts Amendment Act 1890 to public walks and pleasure grounds situated both within and without the district of the authority which can be conveniently used by the inhabitants of the district.

Originally, the 1875 and 1890 Acts applied only to urban sanitary authorities but they were ultimately extended to all local authorities by paragraph 23 of Schedule 14 to the Local Government Act 1972. Such authorities are specified in section 180(1) of, and paragraph 26 of Schedule 14 to, the Local Government Act 1972 and comprise the following:

district councils, London borough councils, the Common Council of the City of London, the Sub-Treasurer of the Inner Temple, the Under Treasurer of the Middle Temple, parish councils in England, and county councils, county borough councils and community councils in Wales.

Bathing places

Section 221 of the Public Health Act 1936, as originally enacted, empowered local authorities to provide baths, washhouses, swimming baths and other swimming places. That part of the section covering swimming baths and places was repealed and effectively replaced by section 19 of the Local Government (Miscellaneous Provisions) Act 1976 (see pages 52–54 below). However, certain provisions in sections 223–229 of the 1936 Act relating to swimming baths remain in force. Under these provisions, a local authority may close them temporarily so as to grant their exclusive use (either free or for payment) to a school or club or to persons organising swimming practices or contests, aquatic sports or other entertainments or may organise such events itself; between 1st October and 30th April it may close the baths and use them or allow them to be used or let for such purpose and subject to such conditions as it thinks fit. There is also power to provide bathing huts and other conveniences for bathing and to charge for them.

Under section 231 of the 1936 Act, a local authority may make byelaws regulating its bathing places and persons resorting thereto: for excluding undesirables and for regulating such matters as bathing times, management of huts and safety. It also has power to make byelaws for places not under the council's management relating to water purity, the adequacy and cleanliness of accommodation, the regulation of those using the baths and the prevention of accidents.

45

Section 17 of the Local Government (Miscellaneous Provisions) Act 1976 empowers a local authority making byelaws regulating public bathing at the seaside to extend the operation of the byelaws to 1,000 metres beyond the low water mark, but subject to the power of the Secretary of State to reduce the area covered by the byelaws so that they do not affect the area of another local authority.

Chapter 5 deals with byelaws.

For the purposes of the 1936 Act, local authorities are defined in section 1(2) as a district council, a London borough council, the Common Council of the City of London, the Sub-Treasurer of the Inner Temple, the Under Treasurer of the Middle Temple in England and a county or a county borough council in Wales. Parish councils in England and community councils in Wales are also designated as local authorities for the purposes of Part VIII of the 1936 Act.

Boating pools and lakes

Section 54 of the Public Health Act 1961 empowers a local authority to provide boating pools and lakes in parks and pleasure grounds provided by it. It may provide such buildings and execute such work as may be necessary or expedient in connection with the provision of boating pools and may also provide boats for the boating pool and such other equipment as may be reasonably required in connection with the use of the boating pool and buildings.

Sections 53 and 54 of the 1961 Act (applying with amendment section 44 of the Public Health Acts Amendment Act 1890) empowers a local authority to provide and let, or license some other person to provide and let, pleasure boats together with the necessary buildings and equipment.

There are some restrictions on the powers of local authorities to provide boating pools, as follows:

(a) where the existence of a boating pool is likely to interfere with any water flowing directly or indirectly out of or into any watercourse which is vested in or controlled by the Environment Agency or any internal drainage board, the local authority must before providing a boating pool under this section consult with that Agency or, as the case may be, that board;

(b) no power given by this section shall be exercised in such a manner as to contravene any covenant or condition subject to which a gift or lease of a park or pleasure ground has been accepted or made without the consent of the donor, grantor, lessor or other person or persons entitled in law to the benefit of the covenant or condition;

(c) section 278 of the Public Health Act 1936 (under which compensation may be paid for damage incurred in consequence of the exercise by the local authority of their powers under that Act) applies;

(d) sections 331 and 334 of the Public Health Act 1936 (which contain savings for water rights and for the works of land drainage authorities) apply;

(e) no local authority is authorised to do anything in contravention of byelaws made by virtue of paragraph 5 of Schedule 25 to the Water Resources Act 1991 or section 66 of the Land Drainage Act 1991.

Section 17 of the 1976 Act (see the previous section) applies to byelaws about boating as well as bathing.

Ice skating

Under section 76 of the Public Health Acts Amendment Act 1907, as amended, a local authority is given power to enclose during time of frost any part of a park or pleasure ground for the purpose of protecting ice for skating, and charge admission to the part inclosed, but only on condition that at least three-quarters of the ice available for the purpose of skating is open to the use of the public free of charge.

Provision of areas for organised sports and associated facilities

Section 76 of the Public Health Acts Amendment Act 1907 empowers a local authority:

(a) to set apart any part of a park or ground as may be fixed by the local authority, and may be described in a notice board affixed or set up in some conspicuous position in the park or ground, for the purpose of cricket, football or any other game or recreation, and to exclude the public from the part set apart while it is in actual use for that purpose;

(b) to provide any apparatus for games and recreations, and charge for the use thereof, or let the right of providing any such apparatus for any term not exceeding three years to any person;

(c) to place, or authorise any person to place, chairs or seats in any such park or ground, and charge for, or authorise any person to charge for, the use of the chairs so provided;

(d) to provide and maintain any reading rooms, pavilions or other buildings and conveniences, and to charge for admission thereto, subject in the case of reading rooms to the limitation that such a charge shall not be made on more than twelve days in any one year, nor on more than four consecutive days;

(e) to provide and maintain refreshment rooms in any such park, and either manage them themselves or, if they think fit, let them to any person for any term not exceeding three years.

The foregoing powers must not be exercised in such a manner as to contravene any covenant or condition subject to which a gift or lease of the park or pleasure ground has been accepted or made, without the consent of the donor, grantor, lessor or other person or persons entitled in law to the benefit of such covenant or condition.

Under section 77 of the Act, the local authority may appoint officers for securing the observance of section 76 of 1907 Act, and of any regulations and byelaws (for byelaws, see Chapter 5) made thereunder, and may procure such officers to be sworn in as constables for that purpose, but any such officer shall not act as a constable unless in uniform or provided with a warrant.

Section 56 of the Public Health Act 1925, as amended, provides that when any part of a park or ground has been set apart by the local authority under section 76 of the 1907 Act for the purpose of cricket, football or any other game or recreation, the local authority may charge reasonable sums for the use thereof for that purpose.

Section 1(3) of the 1925 Act provides that Parts I to VIII of the Act (section 56 is in Part VI) shall be construed as one with the 1907 Act. This means that definitions and expressions in the 1907 Act apply to the 1925 Act without specific enactment and that both Acts must be interpreted as if they were one Act. Whilst this may sometimes raise problems of construction, owing to an inconsistency between Acts, there is unlikely to be any difficulty in this regard with the few provisions of the 1907 and 1925 Acts still in force.

Local authorities covered by sections 76 and 77 are the same as those covered by section 164 of the Public Health Act 1875 and the Public Health Acts Amendment Act 1890 (see above).

Closure of parks and pleasure grounds

Under section 44 of the Public Health Acts Amendment Act 1890 (as amended by section 53 of the Public Health Act 1961), a local authority may close its parks and pleasure grounds for not more than 12 days in the year and grant their use (free or for payment) to any public charity or institution or for any agricultural, horticultural or other show or public purpose, or may use them for any such show or purpose itself, and on closed days admission to the parks, etc. may be free or for such payment as is directed by the authority. Closure may not be imposed on a Sunday, nor for more than six days consecutively, nor may more than a quarter of all the parks, etc. provided by the authority be closed on a Bank Holiday or at Christmas, Good Friday, or a day of public mourning or thanksgiving.

The powers of local authorities to acquire land by purchase or lease are described in Chapter 2. Byelaws are covered in Chapter 5.

Management of open spaces

Section 10 of the Open Spaces Act 1906 provides that a local authority which has acquired any estate or interest in or control over any open space or burial ground under the Act shall, subject to any conditions under which the estate, interest, or control was so acquired:

(a) hold and administer the open space or burial ground in trust to allow, and with a view to, the enjoyment thereof by the public as an open space within the meaning of the Act and under proper control and regulation and for no other purpose; and

(b) maintain and keep the open space or burial ground in a good and decent state.

The authority may inclose it or keep it inclosed with proper railings and gates, and may drain, level, lay out, turf, plant, ornament, light, provide with seats and otherwise improve it, and do all such works and things and employ such officers and servants as may be requisite for those purposes.

'Open space' is defined in section 20 of the 1906 Act as 'any land, whether inclosed or not, on which there are no buildings or of which not more than one twentieth part is covered with buildings, and the whole or the remainder of which is laid out as a garden or is used for the purposes of recreation, or lies waste and unoccupied'.

A burial ground 'includes a churchyard, cemetery, or other ground, whether consecrated or not, which has been at any time set apart for the purpose of interment'.

Under section 11 of the Act, the powers of management may not be exercised in consecrated land until a faculty or licence has been obtained from the bishop. Games may not be played in a burial ground without the consent, in the case of consecrated land, of the bishop (given by licence or faculty) and, in the case of other land, of the person from whom the estate, interest or control was obtained. Any consent may be given subject to conditions.

Section 11 also makes special provision for the removal of monuments and the like. Headstones, tombstones or monuments in a disused burial ground may be moved by a local authority but it must at least three months beforehand prepare a statement sufficiently describing by name, date and other necessary particulars the tombstones and monuments in the ground, and the statement must be open to public inspection. The authority must on three occasions advertise in a newspaper circulating in the area its intention, the existence and place of deposit of the statement and the hours when it is open to inspection and, in addition, it must place a copy of the advertisement on the door of the church (if any) and send a copy by post to any known near relatives. If the ground is consecrated, the council must wait for at least one month after the appearance of the last of the advertisements and must then apply for a faculty or licence to the bishop. No monuments or tombstones in consecrated ground may be moved until such licence or faculty has been obtained.

Section 15 empowers a local authority to make byelaws for the regulation of public behaviour (see Chapter 5 for details).

Local authorities for the purposes of the 1906 Act are county councils, district councils, London borough councils, the Common Council of the City of London and parish councils in England, and county or county borough councils and community councils in Wales.

Recreational facilities generally

Section 19(1) of the Local Government (Miscellaneous Provisions) Act 1976 gives very wide powers to local authorities to provide recreational facilities of all kinds. These include (but without prejudice to the generality of the power):

(a) indoor facilities consisting of sports centres, swimming pools, skating rinks, tennis, squash and badminton courts, bowling centres, dance studios and riding schools;

(b) outdoor facilities consisting of pitches for team games, athletics grounds, swimming pools, tennis courts, cycle tracks, golf courses, bowling greens, riding schools, camp sites and facilities for gliding;

(c) facilities for boating and water-skiing on inland and coastal waters and for fishing in such waters;

(d) premises for the use of clubs or societies having athletic, social or recreational objects;

(e) staff, including instructors, in connection with any such facilities or premises as are mentioned in the preceding paragraphs and in connection with any other recreational facilities provided by the authority;

(f) such facilities in connection with any other recreational facilities as the authority considers it appropriate to provide including facilities by way of parking spaces and places at which food, drink and tobacco may be bought from the authority or another person.

The foregoing also includes powers to provide buildings, equipment, supplies and assistance of any kind.

Under section 19(2), a local authority may make any facilities provided by it in pursuance of section 19(1) available for use by such persons as the authority thinks fit, either without charge or on payment of such charges as the authority thinks fit.

Under section 19(3), a local authority may contribute:

(a) by way of grant or loan towards the expenses incurred or to be incurred by any voluntary organisation in providing any recreational facilities which the authority has power to provide by virtue of subsection (1) of this section; and

(b) by way of grant towards the expenses incurred or to be incurred by any other local authority in providing such facilities.

A 'voluntary organisation' is defined to mean any person carrying on or proposing to carry on an undertaking otherwise than for profit.

Rating of parks and open spaces

Under paragraph 15 of Schedule 5 to the Local Government Finance Act 1988, land which consists of a park is exempt from non-domestic rating, provided that:

(a) it has been provided by, or is under the management of, a 'relevant authority' or two or more relevant authorities acting in combination; and

(b) it is available for free and unrestricted use by members of the public (ignoring any temporary closure at night or in the day).

A park includes a pleasure ground, a public walk, an open space within the meaning of the Open Spaces Act 1906 and a field provided under the Physical Training and Recreation Act 1937. The 1937 Act was repealed by the Local Government (Miscellaneous Provisions) Act 1976 and effectively replaced by section 19 of that Act. However, paragraph 5 of Schedule 15 to the 1988 Act makes no mention of section 19 of the 1976 Act and it is thus unclear whether or not premises and facilities provided by relevant authorities under section 19 enjoy exemption from non-domestic rating.

Relevant authorities are: Ministers of the Crown or government departments or officers exercising functions on behalf of the Crown, local authorities (defined on page xxvii), parish and community councils and the chairmen of parish meetings of parishes in England which do not have councils. Private individuals and non-governmental bodies do not enjoy exemption from non-domestic rates under paragraph 15 of Schedule 5, but may do so under other provisions of the 1988 Act.

Under section 47 of the 1988 Act, a billing authority (defined on page xxvii) has power to grant discretionary relief from the payment of all or some part of non-domestic rates on premises in respect of which:

(a) the ratepayer is a charity or trustees for a charity and the premises are used wholly or mainly for charitable purposes (not necessarily those of the ratepayer charity);

(b) all or part of the premises are occupied for the purposes of one or more non profit-making institutions or organisations whose main objects are charitable or are otherwise philanthropic, or religious or concerned with education, social welfare, science, literature or fine arts;

(c) the ratepayer is a registered community sports club within Schedule 18 to the Finance Act 2002 and the premises are used wholly or mainly for the purposes of that club or that club and another registered club;

(d) the premises are used wholly or mainly for recreational purposes and all or part of the premises are occupied for the purposes of a club, society or other organisation not established or conducted for profit.

The foregoing list is comprehensive enough to cover virtually all non-profit making bodies which own or manage parks and open spaces.

The method of calculating the basic or mandatory rate relief is prescribed in section 43(5) and (6) of the 1988 Act. The calculation produces a reduction of 80%. A billing authority has discretion to increase the reduction to 100%.

Although a park or open space is almost invariably free from the burden of non-domestic rates, facilities provided within the park or open space may be rateable.

The following ancillary facilities have been held to be ancillary to a park and therefore exempt:

- a refreshment pavilion (*Sheffield Corporation v Tranter (VO)* [1957] 2 All ER 583);

- a bandstand, bowling green, residences for park staff and a refreshment kiosk (*Liverpool Corporation v West Derby Assessment Committee* [1908] 2 KB 647);

- changing rooms, a staff mess room, a nursery garden with cottage, a stables and garage and a groundsman's residence (*Bexley Borough Council v Draper* [1954] 47 R & IT 431);

- a miniature railway (*Southern Miniature Railway v Hake (VO)* [1959] 5 RRC 119);

- swimming pools situated within a local authority park, because they were not so carved out of the park as to acquire a distinct and separate status and were used for a purpose which was solely to enhance the attractiveness of the park as a park (*Oxford City Council v Broadway (VO)* [1999] RA 169);

- a country park which was available for free and unrestricted use by the public – charges for parking did not restrict free use of the country park (*Hampshire County Council v Broadway (VO)* [1982] RA 309, [1983] JPL 122);

- an information centre, house, garage and premises, situated 570 yards from a public park and used as the house of the park ranger, as a café run by the ranger's wife, for exhibitions and the display of literature, and other uses related to the park (*Lancashire County Council v Land (VO)* [1987] RA 153).

The following have been held to be separate from the park and therefore rateable:

- swimming baths, open air swimming pool, boating lake, pavilion, lock-up shop and foreshore (*North Riding of Yorkshire County Valuation Committee v Redcar Corporation* [1943] KB 114);

- a swimming pool (*Smith (VO) v St. Albans District Council* [1978] RA 147);

- a bowling green (*Blake (VO) v Hendon Corporation (No. 2)* [1965] 11 RRC 179);

- a restaurant (*London County Council v Robinson (VO)* [1955] 48 R & LT 455);

- two houses occupied by park officials (*Crosby Borough Council v Lyster [1955]* 49 R & IT 23);

- a sports ground owned by trustees of a registered charity, because (i) the section of the public for the benefit of which the ground was dedicated by grant in 1937 was too small to permit it to be said that the ground was occupied by the public, and (ii) the rights of the public to use the ground did not exhaust all possibilities of value to an occupying tenant since there was a power under the trust deed which enabled the management committee to let part of the ground or the whole of it in parts for up the three years on such terms as the committee may determine (*Max Pullan Management Committee v Simpson (VO)* [1989] RA 128);

- an historic mansion situated in a public park (which was exempt) used as an art gallery and museum to which the public were admitted free of charge, because the mansion was not part of the park within which it was situated but was a separate and distinct amenity from the park (*Manchester City Council v Fogg (VO)* [1990] RA 181);

- a cricket clubhouse situated on a recreation ground, because it was not available for free and unrestricted use by members of the public as it was a separate hereditament in the occupation of the taxpayer and did not form part of the recreation ground as a public park (*Galgate Cricket Club v Doyle (VO)* [2001] RA 21).

It will be noted from the above cases that similar facilities have sometimes been held to be rateable and sometimes not. The test is whether or not the facilities are part and parcel of the park or open space which enjoys the exemption.

Chapter 5

REGULATING PUBLIC BEHAVIOUR

Byelaws

Introduction

Byelaws are a form of local law made under the authority of an Act of Parliament which has effect only in a particular area and in relation to a particular activity or group of activities.

Parliament has conferred the power to make byelaws on numerous bodies, including local authorities of all kinds, statutory undertakers (e.g. electricity, gas and water companies), government agencies (e.g. Natural England, the Countryside Council for Wales) and private bodies with public responsibilities (e.g. the National Trust, boards of commons conservators).

This part of the chapter covers the making and enforcement of byelaws by local authorities; the use of these powers by other bodies is outside the scope of the book.

A byelaw is a form of subordinate legislation (i.e. subordinate to Acts of Parliament) and must:

1. Be within the powers of the byelaw-making authority: *Boddington v British Transport Police* [1998] 2 All ER 203 – a byelaw to prohibit smoking in a railway carriage made by the British Railways Board under section 67(1) of the Transport Act 1962 (as amended) was held to be within the statutory power to make byelaws to regulate 'the use and working of, and travel on, [the] railways... with respect to the smoking of tobacco in railway carriages and elsewhere and the

prevention of nuisances'; a claim that the prohibition on smoking in every carriage on a train was beyond the byelaw-making powers of the BRB was rejected by the House of Lords.

2. Not be repugnant to or inconsistent with the general law (both common law and statute): *Powell v May* [1946] KB 330 – a byelaw to prohibit bookmaking in a public place made by Glamorgan County Council was held to be beyond the powers of the council because it was repugnant to the general law of the land as contained in the Street Betting Act 1906 and the Betting and Lotteries Act 1943 [both now repealed].

3. Be certain, by showing clearly what is controlled or prohibited: *Percy & Another v Hall* [1996] 4 All ER 523 – byelaws made by the Secretary of State under the Military Lands Act 1982 to prohibit access to Menwith Hill Station (a military installation) were held to be valid despite uncertainty about the exact border of the area to which access was prohibited.

4. Be reasonable: *Kruse v Johnson* [1898] 2 QB 91 – a byelaw prohibiting any person from playing music or singing in a public place or highway within fifty yards of a dwelling house after being requested by a constable or an inmate of the house was held to be reasonable.

Local authority byelaws – powers
The powers of local authorities to make byelaws in relation to parks, open spaces, recreation grounds and facilities therein are set out in particular statutes and are as follows:

• *Pleasure grounds, public walks and open spaces*: section 164, Public Health Act 1875 and section 15, Open Spaces Act 1906.

- *Pleasure fairs:* section 75, Public Health Act 1961 (as amended by section 22, Local Government (Miscellaneous Provisions) Act 1976).

- *Promenades:* section 83, Public Health Acts Amendment Act 1907.

- *Seashores:* section 82, Public Health Acts Amendment Act 1907.

- *Public bathing:* section 231, Public Health Act 1936 (as amended by section 17, Local Government (Miscellaneous Provisions) Act 1976).

- *Public conveniences:* section 87, Public Health Act 1936.

- *Good rule and government and the prevention and suppression of nuisances:* section 235, Local Government Act 1972. These byelaws can apply to the whole of a local authority area, not only to parks and open spaces.

Local authorities also have powers to provide parking places for cycles and motor vehicles under the Road Traffic Regulation Act 1984.

Procedure for making byelaws
The procedure for making local authority byelaws is set out in section 236 of the LGA 1972. Byelaws have to be confirmed by the confirming authority before they take effect. So far as English local authorities are concerned, the confirming authority for the byelaws mentioned immediately above is the Secretary of State for Communities and Local Government. For Welsh local authorities, that authority in relation to all types of byelaw is the National Assembly.

Section 129 of the Local Government and Public Involvement in Health Act 2007 prospectively adds a new section 236A to the LGA 1972. The new section empowers the Secretary of State in England to make regulations to prescribe classes of byelaw to which section 236 does not apply and to make separate provision for such byelaws. For the purposes of section 236A, the classes of byelaw may be classified in particular by reference to:

(a) the enactment under which the byelaws are made;

(b) the subject matter of the byelaws;

(c) the authority by which the byelaws are made;

(d) the authority or person by whom the byelaws are confirmed.

DCLG has issued a consultation document on the new legislation but, at the time of writing, section 236A had not been brought into force.

For byelaws covering other matters which may be relevant to parks and open spaces, the confirming authorities in England are:

- *Byelaws relating to the countryside* (commons, country parks, National Parks, etc.): DEFRA, Zone 1/03, Temple Quay House, 2 The Square, Temple Quay, Bristol BS1 6EB. Byelaws relating to Nature Reserves recognised by Natural England European Wildlife Division are the responsibility of DEFRA, Nature Reserves Section, Temple Quay House, 2 The Square, Bristol BS1 6EB.

- *Byelaws relating to dogs*: DEFRA, Zone 4/E10, Ashdown House, 123 Victoria Street, London SW1E 6DE.

Byelaws relating to dogs may not be included in byelaws for which the Secretary of State for Communities and Local Government is the confirming authority. Where it is proposed to revoke an existing set of byelaws which include both dog and non-dog byelaws, separate byelaws must be made in respect of the two categories and an application made to DEFRA in respect of those which relate to dogs.

- *Byelaws relating to seaside pleasure boats*: pleasure boats (under section 76 of the Public Health Act 1961, as amended), and pleasure boats and vessels let to hire to the public (under section 185 of the Local Government, Planning and Land Act 1980) are the responsibility of the Maritime & Coastal Agency, Bay 1/11, Spring Place, 105 Commercial Road, Southampton SO15 1EG.

For England, DCLG has issued detailed guidance notes relating to the byelaws for which it is the confirming authority. These can be viewed on and downloaded from the Department's website at www.communities.gov.uk. The National Assembly has not issued any guidance of its own but Welsh local authorities will find that the guidance issued by DCLG is comprehensive.

Enforcement of byelaws
Breach of a byelaw is a summary offence and is dealt with by a magistrates' court. The maximum penalty on conviction is a fine not exceeding the amount fixed by the enactment empowering the making of the byelaw or, where there is no such fixed amount, the sum of level 2 on the standard scale (currently £500). In the case of a continuing offence, the offender may be fined up to £5 per day for each day for which the offence continues after conviction.

Sometimes, a byelaw may provide for enforcement by non-monetary means, e.g. removal from the place to which the byelaw applies. Byelaw 60 of the model byelaws for pleasure grounds provides that a person offending against any byelaw may be removed from the pleasure ground by an officer of the council or by a constable.

If the penalty prescribed by a byelaw does not provide an adequate punishment, the Attorney General may seek an injunction from a civil court to restrain the commission of a breach of the byelaw. Thus, in *A G v Harris* [1960] 3 All ER 207, a flower seller was convicted some 70 times for breach of a byelaw prohibiting the sale of flowers on a highway. The maximum penalty at the time was a fine of £2 and the defendant was willing to pay this. The level of fine was clearly inadequate to deter the commission of the offence and an injunction was obtained. Breach of an injunction is a contempt of court which can be punished by imprisonment.

Model byelaws
DCLG publishes model byelaws on the following topics:

- Pleasure grounds, public walks and open spaces (Model Byelaw 2).

- Amusement premises (Model Byelaw 3).

- Pleasure fairs (Model Byelaw 4).

- Promenades (Model Byelaw 5).

- The seashore (Model Byelaw 6).

- Good rule and government (Model Byelaw 8).

- Markets (Model Byelaw 10).

Subjects for which byelaws are not appropriate
DCLG has issued guidance to the effect that byelaws covering the following subjects, which are or may be relevant to public parks and open spaces, are not appropriate because these are dealt with in general legislation:

- *Advertisements, including notices, posters and bills.* The display of advertisements is regulated by Chapter III of Part VIII of the Town and Country Planning Act 1990, the Town and Country Planning (Control of Advertisements) Regulations 1992 (SI 1992/666) (in relation to Wales only), the Town and Country Planning (Control of Advertisements) (England) Regulations 2007 (SI 2007/783), the Town and Country Planning (Control of Advertisements) (England) (Amendment) Regulations 2007 (SI 2007/1739) and sections 33 and 34 of the Clean Neighbourhoods and Environment Act 2005.

- *Birds, birds' nests, bird eggs.* These are extensively protected under section 1 of the Wildlife and Countryside Act 1981.

- *Camping – removal of campers.* Local authorities are empowered by section 77 of the Criminal Justice and Public Order Act 1994 to direct unauthorised campers to leave the land, and remove their vehicles and any other property.

- *Damage.* A person who, without lawful excuse destroys or damages any property belonging to another, commits an offence under section 1 of the Criminal Damage Act 1971.

- *Dangerous driving in parks and open spaces.* Sections 2 and 3 of the Road Traffic Act 1988 make it an offence to drive dangerously on a road or other public

65

place, or without due care and attention, or without reasonable consideration for other persons using the road or place.

- *Dumping and fly tipping.* A person who without lawful authority abandons on any land in the open air a motor vehicle or any other thing brought for the purpose of abandoning it there commits an offence under section 2 of the Refuse Disposal (Amenity) Act 1978.

- *Firearms.* A person who without lawful authority or reasonable excuse has with him in a public place a loaded shotgun, an air weapon (whether loaded or not), or any other firearm (whether loaded or not) together with ammunition suitable for use in that firearm, or an imitation firearm commits an offence under section 19 of the Firearms Act 1968. Under section 19A of the Firearms Act 1968, it is an offence for any person without lawful authority to carry a small-calibre pistol outside of a licensed pistol club. By virtue of Rule 3(4) of the Firearms Rules 1998 (SI 1998/1941), the holder of a firearm or shotgun certificate must, when the firearm or ammunition or the shotgun is in transit to or from a place in connection with its use, take reasonable precautions for the safe custody of the weapon or ammunition. Failure to do so is an offence under section 1(2) of the Firearms Act 1968 in the case of a firearm and under section 2(2) in the case of a shotgun.

- *Graffiti.* Graffiti is dealt with as damage under the Criminal Damage Act 1971 and under sections 43 and 43A of the Anti-social Behaviour Act 2003.

- *Gypsies and travellers.* Unauthorised camping is an offence under section 77 of the Public Order Act 1994.

Guidance on unauthorised camping can be obtained from the Gypsy & Travellers Unit, Communities and Local Government, 1/F8 Eland House, Bressenden Place, London SW1E 5DU.

- *Language – violent, threatening or abusive.* The use of violent, threatening or abusive language is dealt with under public order legislation.

- *Litter.* A person who leaves litter (including cigarette ends and chewing gum) in any public open place commits an offence under section 87 of the Environmental Protection Act 1990, as amended by the Clean Neighbourhoods and Environment Act 2005. (See Chapter 5 for a detailed discussion.)

- *Public meetings and gatherings.* Part II of the Public Order Act 1986 contains provisions relating to public assemblies.

- *Public order.* A person who uses threatening, abusive or insulting words or behaviour, or disorderly behaviour, within the hearing or sight of a person likely to be caused harassment, alarm or distress commits an offence under section 5 of the Public Order Act 1986.

- *Sale of vehicles on road.* It is an offence under section 3 of the Clean Neighbourhoods and Environment Act 2005 to expose or advertise for sale two or more cars within 500 metres of each other on a public road.

- *Traffic.* Before a byelaw is made to control the use of vehicles, consideration should be given to whether a traffic regulation order made under the Road Traffic Regulation Act 1984 would be more appropriate. Section 2(1) enables an order to be made prohibiting, restricting or regulating the use of a road or any part of the width of a road, including any verges forming part of the road. Section 2(2)(c) allows for the prohibition of, or restriction on, the waiting of vehicles. Section 127 applies the provisions of a traffic regulation order to horses being ridden on footpaths, bridleways and byways open to all traffic, including any road verges or margins that can be so described. Section 34 of the Road Traffic Act 1988 prohibits the driving of any mechanically propelled vehicles without lawful authority on to land not forming part of a road.

Control of dogs

Introduction

There are a large number of statutes and statutory instruments relating to the control of dogs and fouling by dogs, reflecting no doubt the great interest of the public in 'man's best friend'.[1] Set out below are those relevant to parks and open spaces.

Metropolitan Police Act 1839

The 1839 Act applies only to the metropolitan police district (i.e. Greater London, excluding the City of London and the Inner and Middle Temples). Section 54 provides that any person who suffers to be at large any unmuzzled ferocious dog commits an offence and is liable to a penalty of not more than level 2 on the standard scale (currently £500).

Section 61 empowers a metropolitan police constable to destroy any dog or other animal reasonably suspected to be in a rabid state, or which has been bitten by a dog or other animal reasonably suspected to be in a rabid state.

---

[1]   Full details can be found in *The Dog Law Handbook* published by Shaw & Sons.

Section 35(2) of the City of London Police Act 1839 makes similar provision for the City of London.

Dogs Act 1871

Section 2 of the Act empowers a magistrates' court, following a complaint, to make an order directing that a dog is kept under proper control by the owner or destroyed.

Animal Health Act 1981

Section 13 of the Animal Health Act 1981 empowers the Secretary of State to make orders in relation to the following matters:

(a) muzzling of dogs and the keeping of dogs under control;

(b) prescribing and regulating the wearing of collars by dogs whilst in a street or public place;

(c) prevention of worrying of animals by dogs and prevention of straying at night by dogs;

(d) seizure and treatment of dogs where an offence is committed in relation to (c);

(e) prescribing and regulating the seizure, detention and disposal of stray dogs and unmuzzled dogs and the recovery of the expenses of the detention of dogs from their owners.

In exercise of the above powers, the Secretary of State has made the Control of Dogs Order 1992 (SI 1992/901). Article 2 of the Order requires that, subject to specified exceptions, every dog while in a highway or in a place of public resort must wear a collar with the name and address of the owner inscribed on the collar or on a plate or badge attached to it. The exceptions are:

(a) any pack of hounds;

(b) any dog while being used for sporting purposes;

(c) any dog while being used for the capture or destruction of vermin;

(d) any dog while being used for the driving or tending of cattle or sheep;

(e) any dog while being used on official duties by a member of Her Majesty's Armed Forces or HM Revenue and Customs or the police force for any area;

(f) any dog while being used in emergency rescue work; or

(g) any dog registered with the Guide Dogs for the Blind Association.

Under Article 3 of the Order it is an offence for the owner or person in charge of a dog, without lawful authority or excuse, proof of which shall lie on him, to cause or permit the dog to be in a highway or in a place of public resort not wearing a collar as prescribed in Article 2. The penalty on summary conviction is a term of imprisonment not exceeding three months or a fine not exceeding level 5 on the standard scale (currently £5,000), or both (prescribed by section 75 of the Animal Health Act 1981, as substituted by section 13 of the Animal Health Act 2002).

Under Article 4, any dog in respect of which an offence is being committed against the Order may be seized and treated as a stray dog under section 3 of the Dogs Act 1906 or under section 149 of the Environmental Protection Act 1990.

The provisions of the Order are operated by the local authority (defined on page xxvii) (and not by the police force for any area).

Dangerous Dogs Act 1989

The 1989 Act extends the powers of a magistrates' court when it makes an order under section 2 of the Dogs Act 1871 (see above). The court may appoint a person to undertake the destruction of a dog and require the person who has custody of a dog to deliver the dog up for destruction. The court may also make an order disqualifying an owner from having custody of a dog for a period stated in the order. There is a right of appeal to the Crown Court against the making of an order under section 2 of the Dogs Act 1871.

A person who fails to comply with an order under the 1871 Act to keep a dog under proper control or to deliver a dog up for destruction is guilty of an offence and liable on summary conviction to a fine not exceeding level 3 on the standard scale (currently £1,000). The court may also disqualify the person from having custody of a dog for the period stated in the order. After a year, a disqualified person may apply to the magistrates' court for the disqualification to be ended.

A person who has custody of a dog whilst disqualified is guilty of an offence and liable on summary conviction to a fine not exceeding level 5 on the standard scale (currently £5,000).

Environmental Protection Act 1990

Section 149 of the 1990 Act requires every local authority (defined on page xxvii) to appoint an officer to discharge the functions relating to stray dogs conferred on local authorities by the section.

Where the officer believes that a dog found in a public place or on any other land or premises is a stray dog, he must (if practicable) seize and detain the dog but only with the consent of the owner or occupier of the land where the dog is found (other than in a public place).

Where a dog seized by an officer wears a collar with the address of any person attached to or inscribed on it, or the owner of the dog is known, the officer must serve on the person whose address is given on the collar, or on the owner, a notice in writing stating:

(a) that the dog has been seized and where it is being kept; and

(b) that the dog will be liable to be disposed of if it is not claimed within seven clear days after the service of the notice and if the amounts which he would be liable to pay for the expenses of detention are not paid.

A person claiming to be the owner of a dog seized under section 149 is not entitled to have the dog returned to him unless he pays all the expenses incurred by reason of its detention and such further amount as is for the time being prescribed. The current prescribed amount is £25 (prescribed by the Environmental Protection (Stray Dogs) Regulations 1992 (SI 1992/288)).

Where any dog seized under section 149 has been detained for seven clear days after the seizure or, where a notice has been served on the appropriate person, the service of the notice, and the owner has not claimed the dog and paid the amounts due above, the officer may dispose of the dog:

(a) by selling it or giving it to a person who will, in his opinion, care properly for the dog;

(b) by selling it or giving it to an establishment for the reception of stray dogs; or

(c) by destroying it in such a manner as to cause as little pain as possible.

A dog seized under the section must not be sold or given for the purposes of vivisection.

Where a dog is disposed of in the above manner to a person acting in good faith, that person becomes the owner of the dog.

The officer must keep a register containing the prescribed particulars of dogs seized under section 149 and the register must be available for inspection, at all reasonable times, by the public free of charge. The particulars are prescribed by the 1992 Regulations (see above).

The officer must ensure that any dog detained under the section is properly fed and maintained.

The officer may cause a dog detained under this section to be destroyed before the expiration of the period of seven clear days mentioned above where he is of the opinion that this should be done to avoid suffering.

A public place is any highway and any other place to which the public are entitled or permitted to have access.

Section 150 of the 1990 Act provides that any person who finds a stray dog must at once return the dog to its owner or take the dog to the appropriate officer of the local authority for the area in which the dog was found. The finder is allowed to keep the dog if he wishes to do so, subject to compliance with the procedure laid down in the 1992 Regulations. If he keeps the dog, the finder must keep it for at least one month.

Where the finder does not wish to keep the dog, the officer must treat the dog as a stray (unless he has reason to believe that the dog is not a stray).

Failure to comply with the foregoing renders a finder liable on summary conviction to a fine not exceeding level 2 on the standard scale (currently £500).

Dangerous Dogs Act 1991
Under section 1 of the 1991 Act, a person must not allow a dog of a specified dangerous breed (pit bull terrier, Japanese tosa, Dogo Argentino and Fila Braziliero, the latter two being prescribed by the Dangerous Dogs (Designated Types) Order 1991 (SI 1991/1743)), and of which he is the owner or the person in charge, to be in a public place without being muzzled and on a lead. It is also an offence to abandon a dangerous dog or allow it to stray.

Contravention of section 1 is an offence for which the maximum penalty on summary conviction is a term of imprisonment not exceeding six months or a fine not exceeding level 5 on the standard scale (currently £5,000), or both.

Under section 3 of the 1991 Act, if a dog is dangerously out of control in a public place, the owner and (if different) the person in charge of the dog is guilty of an offence. If the dog injures anyone while out of control, the owner, etc. is guilty of an aggravated offence. It is a defence for an owner who was not at the relevant time in charge of the dog to prove that the dog was at that time in the charge of a person reasonably believed by the owner to be a fit and proper person to be in charge of the dog.

A person guilty of an offence under the section is liable on summary conviction to a term of imprisonment not exceeding six months or a fine not exceeding level 5 on the standard scale (currently £5,000), or both. A person guilty of an aggravated offence is liable on summary conviction to imprisonment for a term not exceeding six months or a fine not exceeding the statutory maximum (currently £5,000, prescribed under section 32(9) of the Magistrates' Courts Act 1980) and on conviction on indictment to a term of imprisonment not exceeding two years or a fine, or both.

In *R v Bezzina, R v Codling, R v Elvin* [1994] 3 All ER 964, the three defendants were each accused of being the owner of a dog which was dangerously out of control in a public place and which while out of control injured a person, contrary to section 3(1). They were convicted and appealed on the ground that the offence was not one of strict liability. The Court of Appeal rejected their argument and held that Parliament had not intended to introduce an element of *mens rea* and the offence was one of strict liability.

Where a person is convicted of an offence under sections 1 or 3 of the 1991 Act, the court may order the destruction of the dog in respect of which the offence was committed and must do so in the case of an aggravated offence (except where the court is satisfied that the dog would not be a danger to public safety or in some cases where the dog was born before 30th November 1991). The court may also disqualify a convicted person from having custody of a dog for such period as the court thinks fit. In both cases, there is a right of appeal to the Crown Court. Breach of a disqualification order is an offence for which the penalty on summary conviction is a fine not exceeding level 5 on the standard scale (currently £5,000).

Clean Neighbourhoods and Environment Act 2005, Part 6
Section 55 empowers a primary authority and a secondary authority to make an order providing for an offence or offences in relation to the control of dogs in its area. A primary authority is a district council in England, a county

council in England for an area for which there are no district councils, a London borough council, the Common Council of the City of London, the Council of the Isles of Scilly and a Welsh county or county borough council. A secondary authority is a parish council in England and a community council in Wales.

A dog control order may relate to one or more of the following:

(a) fouling of land by dogs and the removal of dog faeces;

(b) keeping of dogs on leads;

(c) exclusion of dogs from land;

(d) the number of dogs which a person may take on to any land.

Section 56 requires the Secretary of State to make regulations prescribing the penalties for breach of a dog control order (which cannot exceed level 3 on the standard scale) and prescribing the form and content of a dog control order. The relevant regulations for England are the Dog Control Orders (Prescribed Offences and Penalties etc.) Order 2006 (SI 2006/798) and the Dog Control Orders (Procedures) Order 2006 (SI 2006/798) and, for Wales, the Dog Control Orders (Miscellaneous Provisions) (Wales) Regulations 2007 (SI 2007/702).

Section 57 provides that dog control orders may only apply to land in the open air to which the public are entitled or permitted to have access with or without payment. Covered land is in the open air if it is open to the air on at least one side. The Secretary of State may designate land which is not to be subject to dog control orders. The relevant regulations are the Controls on Dogs (Non-application to Designated Land) Order 2006 (SI 2006/779) (England) and the Controls on Dogs (Non-application to Designated Land) (Wales) Order 2007 (SI 2007/701). Both Orders designate Forestry Commission land and land over which a road passes. Where land is regulated under a private Act otherwise than by a primary or a secondary authority, the person who has the powers of regulation may by notice in writing to those authorities in whose area the land is situated exclude the land from the ambit of Part 6.

Section 59 empowers an authorised officer of a primary or secondary authority to issue a fixed penalty notice where he has reason to believe an offence has been committed under a dog control order made by the authority. In addition, such an officer of a secondary authority may issue a fixed penalty notice where he has reason to believe an offence has been committed under a dog control order made by a primary authority. The amount of the fixed penalty is the amount specified by the authority (which may differ for different offences) or, if none, £75. The Secretary of State has power to prescribe maximum and minimum penalty amounts. In England, the Environmental Offences (Fixed Penalties) (Miscellaneous Provisions) Regulations 2007 (SI 2007/175) and, in Wales, the Environmental Offences (Fixed Penalties) (Miscellaneous Provisions) (Wales) Regulations 2007 (SI 2007/739) prescribe £80 and £50, and £150 and £75, respectively as the maximum and minimum amounts.

Where a primary or a secondary authority has byelaws which make similar provision to a dog control order under section 55 of Part 6 of the Act, the byelaws cease to have effect in relation to any land once it becomes subject to a dog control order.

DEFRA has issued guidance on dog control in its publication *Dog Control Orders*. It has also issued particular guidance to parish councils in its publication *Getting to grips with the Clean Neighbourhoods and Environment Act 2005 – a parish council guide to environmental enforcement*. The Welsh Assembly has not issued any specific guidance on dog control orders but the guidance from DEFRA will no doubt be as relevant in Wales as in England.

Control of alcohol

Licensing Act 1872

It is an offence under section 12 of the Licensing Act 1872 to be found drunk in any highway or other public place. An on-the-spot penalty of £40 is payable in accordance with the provisions of Chapter 1 of the Criminal Justice and Police Act 2001 (see the section 'Anti-social behaviour' for details). If the person is tried for the offence, the penalty on summary conviction is a fine not exceeding level 1 on the standard scale.

Criminal Justice Act 1967

Under section 91(1) of the Criminal Justice Act 1967, a person who, whilst drunk, is guilty of disorderly behaviour is liable to pay an on-the-spot penalty of £40 in accordance with the provisions of Chapter 1 of the Criminal Justice and Police Act 2001. If the person is tried for the offence, the penalty on summary conviction is a fine not exceeding level 3 on the standard scale.

Confiscation of Alcohol (Young Persons) Act 1997

This Act empowers a constable to require a person in a relevant place to surrender any alcohol in his possession and any container for alcohol provided that:

(a) the person is under 18; or

(b) the person intends that the alcohol shall be consumed by a person under 18 in that relevant place or another relevant place; or

(c) a person under 18 who is, or recently has been, with that person has recently consumed alcohol in that relevant place or another relevant place.

A constable cannot require the surrender of a sealed container unless he believes that the person is or has been consuming, or intends to consume, alcohol in a relevant place.

A relevant place is a public place (other than licensed premises) or any other place to which the person has unlawfully gained access.

The penalty for failing to comply with a constable's requirement without reasonable excuse is, on summary conviction, a fine not exceeding level 2 on the standard scale.

Criminal Justice and Police Act 2001
Chapter 2 of the Criminal Justice and Police Act 2001 (consumption of alcohol in designated public places) contains provisions for combating alcohol-related disorder.

Section 12 makes it an offence to fail to comply, without a reasonable excuse, with a requirement by a constable not to consume alcohol in a designated public place and to surrender anything containing alcohol. The penalty on summary conviction is a fine not exceeding level 2 on the standard scale.

A place is designated if it is identified in an order made by the local authority in accordance with the Local

Authorities (Alcohol Consumption in Designated Public Places) Regulations 2007 (SI 2007/806).

Section 14 provides that certain places are not public places for the purposes of the Act. They are primarily licensed premises and clubs.

The relevant local authorities in England are unitary authorities and district councils and, in Wales, county and county borough councils.

Licensing Act 2003
Under Part 7 of the Licensing Act 2003 (replacing provisions in the wholly repealed Licensing Act 1964), a large number of offences are created for breach of licensing laws. These include: selling alcohol to children under 18 (section 146); allowing the sale of alcohol to children under 18 (section 147); purchase of alcohol by or on behalf of children under 18 (section 149); delivering alcohol to children under 18 (section 151); sending a child under the age of 18 to obtain alcohol (section 152).

Litter
Introduction
There are detailed provisions, mainly in the Environmental Protection Act 1990, relating to the control of litter on highways, places of public resort, statutory undertakers' land, railway land and land managed by educational institutions.

This part of the chapter only deals with litter in parks and open spaces and references to other types of land in the legislation are generally omitted, unless this is impracticable.

Litter Act 1983

Section 5 empowers a litter authority to provide litter bins in any street or public place. The litter authorities are: county councils, district councils, county and county borough councils in Wales, London borough councils, the Common Council of the City of London, parish and community councils, joint bodies constituted by two or more of the foregoing authorities, the Sub-Treasurer of the Inner Temple and the Under Treasurer of the Middle Temple.

A litter authority is under an obligation to arrange for the regular emptying and cleansing of litter bins provided by it under the 1983 Act. A litter authority may put up notices about the leaving of litter, both in relation to bins provided under the Highways Act 1980 and the 1983 Act, and may erect notice boards for this purpose.

A litter authority may not put any litter bin or notice board on land forming part of an open space within the meaning of the Open Spaces Act 1906 (see Chapter 4) which is managed by another litter authority or parish meeting without the consent of that authority or meeting. A litter authority is similarly constrained in relation to any other land not forming part of a street (e.g. a privately owned open space).

A person who wilfully removes or otherwise interferes with a litter bin or notice board is liable on summary conviction to a fine not exceeding level 1 on the standard scale.

Environmental Protection Act 1990

Part IV of the Environmental Protection Act 1990 (as amended) contains the major portion of the law relating to litter and places primary responsibility for the control of litter in highways, and other areas of land to which the public have access, on the appropriate local authority. In addition, the legislation provides that the owners and occupiers of land can be required to keep their land free from litter.

Section 86 defines the relevant litter authorities, certain types of land, and other matters, as follows:

'Principal litter authority': a county council, a county borough council, a district council, a London borough council, the Common Council of the City of London and the Council of the Isles of Scilly.

'Relevant land' of a principal litter authority is land open to the air which is under the direct control of the authority and to which the public are entitled or permitted to have access, with or without payment.

'Relevant land' of a 'designated educational institution' is land in the open air under the direct control of the governing body of an educational institution designated by the Secretary of State. The designated bodies include universities and other further education establishments, community foundation and voluntary schools and city technology colleges, but not independent (fee-paying) schools.

'Relevant land' of a 'designated statutory undertaker' is land under the direct control of any statutory undertaker, as defined in the Environmental Protection Act 1990 or as designated by the Secretary of State, to which the public are entitled or permitted to have access with or without payment or, in prescribed cases, land to which the public have no right of, or consent to, access. The Secretary of State has prescribed in the Litter (Statutory Undertakers) (Designation and Relevant Land) Order 1991 (SI 1991/1043, as amended) the types of statutory undertaker and the types of land for the purposes of Part IV of the 1990 Act. A 'designated statutory undertaker' is a person or body authorised by statute to carry on a railway, road transport, canal, inland navigation, port or airport undertaking.

'Relevant Crown land' is land occupied by a government department, the armed forces or other agency of the Crown which is open to the air and to which the public are entitled or permitted to have access, with or without payment.

Litter includes both litter and refuse, except in relation to the offence of leaving litter and the associated fixed penalty notice system (see pages 87–88 below for details). By virtue of the Litter (Animal Droppings) Order 1991 (SI 1991/961) refuse includes dog faeces on the following types of land:

(a) a public walk or pleasure ground;

(b) any land used as a public garden or recreation area on which there are no buildings or of which buildings cover no more than one twentieth part;

(c) any part of the seashore which is frequented by large numbers of people and which is managed as a tourist resort or recreational facility;

(d) an esplanade or promenade above high tide level;

(e) a picnic site provided by a local planning authority.

Under section 98(5A) of the Act (inserted by section 27 of CNEA 2005), the discarded ends of cigarettes, cigars and like products and discarded chewing gum and the discarded remains of other products designed for chewing are designated as litter.

The responsibility for keeping land free from litter and refuse is prescribed in section 89 as follows:

(a) a principal litter authority in respect of its relevant land;

(b) the appropriate Crown authority as respects its relevant Crown land;

(c) each designated statutory undertaker as respects its relevant land;

(d) the governing body of each designated educational institution, or the education authority responsible for the management of the institution, as the case may be, as respects its relevant land.

Section 89 also requires the Secretary of State to issue a code of practice giving practical guidance on the discharge of the duties described above. The current *Code of Practice on Litter and Refuse* is available from DEFRA.

Section 91 empowers a person (other than a principal litter authority) to make a complaint to a magistrates' court on the ground that he is aggrieved by the defacement by litter of any of the types of relevant land defined above. 'Person' includes a body corporate. Proceedings are brought against the person or body whose duty it is to keep the land in question free of litter. Before beginning proceedings, the complainant must give the person or body at least five days' written notice of his intention to do so; the notice must specify the matter complained of. If the magistrates' court convicts the defendant, it may make a litter abatement order requiring them to clear up the litter within the time specified in the notice. Failure to comply with the notice renders a convicted person liable to the same maximum fines as on conviction for breach of a litter abatement notice (see next paragraph). If charged with this offence, it is a defence to prove that the duty to keep the land as far as practicable free from litter has been complied with. The code of practice is admissible in evidence in any proceedings. If, on hearing a complaint, the court is satisfied that the land was defaced or unclean, and that there were reasonable grounds for bringing the complaint, it must order the defendant to pay the reasonable expenses of the complainant of bringing the matter before the court.

Section 92 provides that, where a principal litter authority (other than an English county council) is satisfied that any relevant Crown land, any relevant land of a designated statutory undertaker or a designated educational institution, or any relevant land within a litter control area is defaced by litter or that defacement is likely to recur, it is under a duty to serve a litter abatement notice. The notice must do one or both of the following:

(a) require that the litter is cleared within a specified time;

(b) prohibit allowing the land to become defaced by litter.

The notice must be served on the Crown authority, or the designated body, or on the occupier of the land; if the land is unoccupied, the notice must be served on the owner. A person served with a litter abatement notice may appeal against it to a magistrates' court within 21 days after the date of service of the notice. The appeal must be allowed if the person proves that he has complied with his duty to ensure as far as practicable that the land is kept free of litter.

If a person served with a litter abatement notice fails without reasonable excuse to comply with it, he is guilty of an offence and liable on summary conviction to a maximum fine of level 4 on the standard scale; he is also liable to a further fine of one twentieth of that level for each day on which the offence continues after conviction. If charged with this offence, it is a defence to prove that the duty to keep the land as far as practicable free from litter has been complied with. The code of practice is admissible in evidence in any proceedings.

If a person fails to comply with a litter abatement notice, the principal litter authority (other than an English county council) may, except in the case of relevant Crown land or relevant land of statutory undertakers, enter the land, clear up the litter and recover any necessary expenditure in so doing from the person.

Sections 92A to 92C (added by section 20 of CNEA 2005) make provision for litter clearing notices. Section 92A empowers principal litter authorities to issue litter clearing notices on the occupiers of land in the open air which they think are defaced by litter or refuse so as to be detrimental to the amenity of the area. Section 92A(11) provides that a litter clearing notice may not be served in relation to the following types of land:

(a) land under the direct control of a principal litter authority;

(b) Crown land;

(c) relevant land of a statutory undertaker (defined above, page 82);

(d) relevant land of a designated educational institution (defined above, page 82).

In discharging their functions under section 92A, principal litter authorities must have regard to guidance issued by the Secretary of State, who is responsible for prescribing the form and content of a litter clearing notice. Guidance is contained in the *Code of Practice on Litter and Refuse* (see page 84 above), but no prescribed form of notice has been issued.

Section 92B gives a person served with a litter clearing notice the right to appeal to a magistrates' court.

Section 92C makes it an offence, without reasonable excuse, to fail to comply with a litter clearing notice. The penalty on summary conviction is a fine not exceeding level 4 on the standard scale. Where a person fails to comply with a notice, the principal litter authority may enter the land and clear it of litter and refuse. The authority may charge the cost to that person.

It is an offence under section 87, as amended by section 18 of CNEA 2005, to throw down, drop or otherwise deposit any litter in any place (whether on land or in water) in the area of a principal litter authority which is open to the air, so long as the public have access to it, with or without payment. No offence is committed where the depositing of litter is authorised by law or is done with the consent of the owner, occupier or other person having control of the place where it is deposited. Where litter is deposited in a lake, pond or watercourse with the consent of the owner, etc. of land, that person may only give consent if he owns, occupies or has control over all the land adjoining the lake, etc. and all the land through which the water in the lake discharges (otherwise than into a public sewer).

A public open place is a place in the open air to which the public are entitled or permitted to have access with or without payment; a covered place is open to the air so long as at least one side is so open and the place is available for public use.

A person guilty of the foregoing offence is liable on summary conviction to a maximum fine of level 4 on the standard scale. A local authority may publicise the penalty for dropping litter.

Section 88 empowers an authorised officer of a principal litter authority who finds a person he believes has just committed the offence of dropping litter to give notice to that person offering an opportunity of discharging any liability to conviction for that offence by payment of a fixed penalty. The amount of the fixed penalty is the amount specified by a principal litter authority in relation to its area or, if no such amount is specified, £75.

Section 19 of CNEA 2005 amends section 88 so as to empower an authorised officer of a litter authority to require a person to whom he intends to give a fixed penalty notice to give his name and address. Failure to do so, or to give false particulars, is an offence for which the penalty on summary conviction is a fine not exceeding level 3 on the standard scale. However, at the time of publication, this section was not in force.

Section 19 of CNEA 2005 further amends section 88 to include parish and community councils as litter authorities with power to issue fixed penalty notices for dropping litter. The Secretary of State has power to prescribe conditions to be applied to a parish or community council in relation to the authorisation of persons to give fixed penalty notices in accordance with section 88. These conditions have been prescribed in the Environmental Offences (Fixed Penalties) (Miscellaneous Provisions)

Regulations 2007 (SI 2007/175) and Environmental Offences (Fixed Penalties) (Miscellaneous Provisions) (Wales) Regulations 2007 (SI 2007/739) and require an authorised person to have successfully completed an approved course of training by an approved training provider.

Firearms and other weapons
Firearms
Section 19 of the Firearms Act 1968 makes it an offence without lawful authority or reasonable excuse for a person to have in a public place:

(a) a loaded shotgun;

(b) an air weapon (loaded or unloaded);

(c) any other firearm (loaded or unloaded) together with ammunition suitable for use in that firearm;

(d) an imitation firearm.

The burden of proof as to whether or not a person has lawful authority or a reasonable excuse lies with that person.

Section 57(1) of the 1968 Act defines a public place as any highway and any other premises or place to which at the material time the public have or are permitted to have access, whether on payment or otherwise. This definition clearly includes a public park, open space, recreation ground and similar places.

Crossbows
Under section 3 of the Crossbows Act 1987, a person under 17 who has with him a crossbow which is capable of

discharging a missile, or parts of a crossbow which, when assembled, is so capable is guilty of an offence unless he is under the supervision of a person aged 21 or over. The offence only applies to crossbows with a draw weight exceeding 1.4 kilograms.

Knives

Under section 139 of the Criminal Justice Act 1988, it is an offence for a person to have with him in a public place any article which has a pointed blade or is sharply pointed except a folding pocketknife with a blade not exceeding three inches. It is a defence under the section for a person to prove that he had good reason or lawful authority to have the article in a public place. Good reasons specified in the section are use for work, religious reasons and being part of a national costume.

The section defines a public place to include any place to which at the material time the public have or are permitted to have access, whether on payment or otherwise. This definition clearly includes a public park, open space, recreation ground and similar places. In *R v Roberts* [2003] EWCA Crim 2753, the Court of Appeal quashed the conviction of a man for a breach of section 139. The Crown Court judge had held that a metre-wide front garden of a terraced house was a public place because a person in the garden could reach out and use a knife on a passing pedestrian. The Court of Appeal ruled that this was an incorrect interpretation of 'public place'.

Offensive weapons

Under section 1 of the Prevention of Crime Act 1953, it is an offence without lawful authority or reasonable excuse for a person to have in a public place any offensive weapon.

The section defines a public place as any highway and any other premises or place to which at the material time the public have or are permitted to have access, whether on payment or otherwise. This definition clearly includes a public park, open space, recreation ground and similar places.

The section defines an offensive weapon as any article made or adapted for use for causing injury to the person, or intended by the person having it with him for such use by him or by some other person.

Anti-social behaviour

Introduction

The control of anti-social behaviour has been the subject of legislation for a very long time. The oldest statute still in force dates from 1824. The Public Order Act 1986 deals with riot, violent disorder, affray, fear or provocation of violence; intentional harassment, alarm or distress; and harassment, alarm or distress. Whilst these activities may occur in parks and open spaces, there is nothing specific in the Act relating to the commission of public order offences in such areas.

The Protection from Harassment Act 1997 makes it an offence to pursue a course of conduct which amounts to harassment of another person. Harassment is not defined in the Act, so that it falls to the courts to interpret the word. Again, this Act is of general application and has no particular reference to parks or open spaces.

Accordingly, this book does not cover the 1986 Act or the 1997 Act in detail.

Vagrancy Act 1824

Under section 4 of the Act, a person committing any one of the offences specified in the section may be summarily convicted and fined an amount not exceeding level 3 on the standard scale and may be imprisoned for up to 14 days. Where the magistrates' court comprises a single Justice or sits in an occasional courthouse, the maximum fine is £1.

The main offences specified in section 4 are: wandering abroad in, *inter alia*, the open air and not giving a good account of oneself; wilfully, openly, lewdly and obscenely exposing one's person with intent to insult a female; being found in a dwelling house, warehouse, stable or outhouse, or in any inclosed yard, garden or area for an unlawful purpose; being apprehended as an idle and disorderly person and violently resisting a constable apprehending him or her.

The Crime and Disorder Act 1998

Section 1(1) (as amended by section 61 of the Police Reform Act 2002) defines anti-social behaviour as behaviour which would enable application to be made for an Anti-Social Behaviour Order against a person (who must be over the age of 10) on the ground that:

(a) the person has acted in an anti-social manner, that is to say, in a manner that caused or was likely to cause harassment, alarm or distress to one or more persons not of the same household as himself; and

(b) that such an order is necessary to protect relevant persons from further anti-social acts by him.

'Relevant persons' are elaborately defined in section 1(1B) to comprise people living in the local government area or the police area, being on or in the vicinity of premises policed by the British Transport Police or being on or in the vicinity of premises provided or managed by a social landlord.

A 'relevant authority' (defined in section 1(1A), added by section 61 of the Police Reform Act 2002) is the council for a local government area (i.e. a district council, a county council (further added by section 85 of the Anti-social Behaviour Act 2003), a London borough council, the City of London, the Council of the Isle of Wight and the Council of the Isles of Scilly in England and a county or a county borough in Wales). The authority may apply to a magistrates' court for an Anti-Social Behaviour Order where behaviour within the definition above is alleged to have occurred. If the authority proves its case, the court may make an order (but is not obliged to do so) which prohibits the defendant from doing anything described in the order. This could include excluding the defendant from an area – such as a park or open space – for a defined period. An order lasts for at least two years, unless the parties agree to a shorter period. Breach of an order is an offence, for which the penalty on summary conviction is a term of imprisonment not exceeding six months or a fine not exceeding the statutory maximum, or both, and the maximum penalty on conviction on indictment is a term of imprisonment not exceeding five years or a fine, or both.

Under section 1B (also added by section 61 of the Police Reform Act 2002), where a relevant authority is a party to any proceedings in a county court, it may apply for what is in effect an Anti-Social Behaviour Order to be imposed on another party to the proceedings if it proves to the court that the other party has indulged in behaviour which falls within section 1(1) (see above). A relevant authority which is not a party to such proceedings may apply to be joined in the proceedings with a view to seeking such an order.

Under section 1C (added by section 64 of the Police Reform Act 2002), where a person is convicted of a 'relevant offence' (i.e. any offence committed after 2nd December 2002, the date on which section 64 came into force), the court may make what is in effect an Anti-Social Behaviour Order if it considers that the offender has acted in an anti-social manner (as defined in section 1(1) – see above) and that the order is necessary to protect persons anywhere in England and Wales from further anti-social acts by him.

Before applying for an order under either section 1(1) or section 1B, the council for a local government area must consult the chief officer of police for the area and *vice versa*.

The Criminal Justice and Police Act 2001 – on-the-spot penalties

The Criminal Justice and Police Act 2001 enacts legislation covering on-the-spot penalties for disorderly behaviour, the combating of alcohol-related disorder, provisions relating to the placing of advertisements by prostitutes and to child curfew schemes.

Section 1 lists offences which are subject to the imposition of a penalty on the spot by a constable. They are called 'penalty offences' in the legislation. The list includes:

(a) being drunk in a highway, other public place or licensed premises;

(b) consumption of alcohol in a designated public place;

(c) depositing or leaving litter;

(d) behaviour likely to cause harassment, alarm or distress;

(e) disorderly conduct while drunk in a public place;

(f) destroying or damaging property.

Where a constable believes that a person aged 18 or over has committed an offence listed above, he may give the offender a penalty notice offering the offender the opportunity of paying a penalty instead of being prosecuted for the offence.

The amount of the penalty is prescribed by the Penalties for Disorderly Behaviour (Amount of Penalty) Order 2002 (SI 2002/1837) (as amended). For offences (a)–(c) above the amount is £50 (£30 for persons under 16) and for (d)–(f) the amount is £80 (£40 for persons under 16).

A person who is given a penalty notice may ask to be tried for the alleged offence, in which case proceedings may be taken against him.

Travellers and gypsies
Unauthorised camping
Section 77 of the Criminal Justice and Public Order Act 1994 empowers a local authority (in England, a county council, district council, London borough council, the Common Council of the City of London and the Council of the Isles of Scilly; in Wales, a county or county borough council) to direct persons residing unlawfully in vehicles within the authority's area on highway land, other unoccupied land or land occupied without the consent of the occupier, to leave the land and to remove their vehicles and any other property they have with them on the land. A person who fails to comply with a direction as soon as practicable commits an offence. It is also an offence for a person who has been directed to leave land to re-enter the land with a vehicle within three months of the date of the

direction. The maximum penalty on conviction is a fine not exceeding level 3 on the standard scale. It is a defence to show that failure to comply with a direction, or returning to the land within three months, was due to mechanical breakdown, illness or other immediate emergency.

Section 78 of the 1994 Act provides that, on a complaint being made by a local authority, a magistrates' court may make an order requiring the removal from the land of any vehicle and property and any person residing in it and may authorise the authority to enter the land and remove the vehicle and property. It is an offence to obstruct anyone who has been authorised to carry out the order, for which the maximum penalty on conviction is a fine not exceeding level 3 on the standard scale.

General advice to local authorities on the provisions of the 1994 Act covering unauthorised camping is given in the DCLG publication *Guidance on Managing Unauthorised Camping*. This is currently out of print but can be viewed on the DCLG's website: www.communities.gov.uk.

General advice
In May 2007, DCLG issued general advice for local authorities in its publication *Local Authorities and Gypsies and Travellers: a guide to responsibilities and powers*. This can also be viewed on the DCLG website: www.communities.gov.uk.

Chapter 6

HEALTH AND SAFETY

Introduction

This chapter covers both statutory provisions relating specifically to health and safety – mainly in the Health and Safety at Work etc. Act 1974 and subordinate legislation made under the Act – and the law relating to occupiers' liability.

The Health and Safety at Work etc. Act 1974

The Health and Safety at Work etc. Act 1974 is a wide-ranging Act, Part I of which is primarily concerned with the health and safety of employees. However, section 3 of the Act imposes on employers and on self-employed persons a duty to conduct their undertakings in such a way as to ensure, so far as is reasonably practicable, that persons not in their employment who may be affected thereby are not exposed to risks to their health and safety. Thus persons (including corporate bodies such as local authorities) providing recreational facilities, public parks, playgrounds and open spaces for public enjoyment are subject to the statutory duty.

Under section 15 of the Act, the Secretary of State may make regulations to supplement the basic statutory duty. A large number of such regulations have been made. None apply specifically to parks, open spaces or playgrounds but the Management of Health and Safety at Work Regulations 1999 (SI 1999/3242, as amended by SI 2005/1541, SI 2006/438, SI 2006/457 and SI 2007/320) are relevant. These Regulations, among many other things, require employers and self-employed persons to make assessments of the health and safety risks to which their respective undertakings give rise, for the purpose of ascertaining what they have to do to comply with their obligations under health and safety legislation. The Regulations also make provision for the review and recording of the results of risk assessments.

Enforcement of the Act is primarily the responsibility of the Health and Safety Executive (www.hse.gov.uk). The Executive has issued advice on health and safety in children's playgrounds, European standards for playground equipment and managing risk in play provision.

Section 47(1) of the Act provides that nothing in Part I is to be construed as conferring a right to take civil action for a breach of section 3. However, section 47(2) provides that breach of a duty imposed by health and safety regulations is actionable insofar as the breach causes damage, unless the regulations specify otherwise. Article 22 of the 1999 Regulations, as substituted by Article 2 of the Management of Health and Safety at Work (Amendment) Regulations 2006 (SI 2006/438), provides that, in relation to the duties of an employee under the 1999 Regulations, a breach of a duty imposed on an employer by the Regulations does not confer a right of action in any civil proceedings insofar as that duty applies for the protection of a third party (i.e. any person other than an employer or an employee). This is a very limited exception to the general rule and probably of little relevance to the use of parks, etc. by members of the public.

Section 16 of the Act empowers the Health and Safety Commission to issue codes of practice to assist those affected by the Act or the regulations made under the Act. Many such codes have been issued but none apply directly to parks and open spaces.

Playground safety

Whilst there are no specific codes of practice for playgrounds issued by the Health and Safety Commission, there is a great deal of non-statutory advice and information. The main sources are:

1. BSI Group (formerly the British Standards Institution) (www.bsi-global.com) has issued many standards relating to playground equipment and safety. Full details are available on the BSI's website.

2. Fields in Trust (formerly the National Playing Fields Association) (www.fieldsintrust.org) have several publications covering all aspects of playgrounds, including *Playground Management and Safety, the Six Acre Standard* (about the minimum desirable play and recreation space per 1,000 inhabitants) and *Insurance and Children's Play.*

3. The Royal Society for the Prevention of Accidents (RoSPA) (www.rospa.com/playsafety) provides extensive information and guidance on play safety.

Occupiers' liability

Occupiers' Liability Act 1957
Under section 2 of the Occupiers' Liability Act 1957, an occupier of premises owes a duty of care (called 'the common duty of care') to all his visitors except insofar as he is free to, and does, extend, restrict, modify or exclude that duty by agreement or otherwise. The occupier of premises is usually the person who has control of the premises. In the case of public parks and open spaces, the occupier is almost invariably the local authority which owns and/or manages them, although some parks and open spaces are owned or managed by charitable trustees,

boards of conservators or other *ad hoc* bodies. A visitor is a person who is invited or permitted by the occupier to enter premises. Premises include not only land but also buildings and other movable or immovable structures (e.g. playground equipment).

The common duty of care is 'to take such care as in all the circumstances of the case is reasonable to see that the visitor will be reasonably safe in using the premises for the purposes for which he is invited or permitted by the occupier to be there' (section 2(2) of the 1957 Act). An occupier must be prepared for children to be less careful than adults and an occupier may expect that a person in exercise of his calling will appreciate and guard against any special risks ordinarily incident to it so far as the occupier leaves him free to do so. Thus, for example, a window cleaner can be expected to take proper care when leaning out of a window to clean the glass. In the context of recreation, a golfer can be expected to take reasonable care to see that no-one is in the way when he plays a shot.

In relation to children, an example of the dangers against which an occupier of premises needs to guard is illustrated by *Glasgow Corporation v Taylor* [1922] 1 AC 44, in which the House of Lords held the Corporation liable where a child died after eating brightly coloured berries from a plant growing in the Corporation's park without knowing that the berries were poisonous.

In determining whether the occupier of premises has discharged the common duty of care to a visitor, regard is to be had to all the circumstances, so that, for example:

(a) where damage is caused to a visitor by a danger of which he has been warned by the occupier, the warning must be adequate (e.g. a written notice must be readily visible and understandable) if the occupier is to be absolved from liability; and

(b) where damage is caused to a visitor by a danger due to the faulty execution of any work of construction, maintenance or repair by an independent contractor employed by the occupier, the occupier is generally not liable for the danger if in all the circumstances he had acted reasonably in entrusting the work to an independent contractor and had taken such steps (if any) as he reasonably ought in order to satisfy himself that the contractor was competent and the work had been properly done.

The common duty of care does not impose on an occupier any obligation to a visitor in respect of risks willingly accepted as his by the visitor. People who enter a park or playing field for any purpose in the exercise of a right conferred by law are to be treated for the purposes of the 1957 Act as permitted to be there for that purpose, whether in fact they have the occupier's permission or not.

In the leading case of *Jolley (AP) v Sutton London Borough Council* [2000] 3 All ER 409, a boat was left abandoned on land owned by Sutton LBC next to a block of flats. Sutton was aware of the boat and made plans to remove it, but these were never implemented. The boat appeared to be sound but was in fact rotten. Two boys, J and his friend K, aged 13 and 14, began to repair the boat and used a car jack and some wood to prop it up. The boat fell off the prop and crushed J, causing such serious spinal injuries that J became quadriplegic. J sued Sutton in negligence and for breach of statutory duty under the 1957 Act. The court of first instance upheld J's claim but reduced the damages by 25% due to J's contributory negligence. The

Court of Appeal overturned this judgment on the ground that Sutton could not have foreseen that J would prop up the boat with a jack. On further appeal, the House of Lords reversed the Court of Appeal and restored the decision of the court of first instance. The House held that whether or not the injury to J was reasonably foreseeable was a question of fact. 'Reasonably foreseeable' was not a fixed point on a scale of probability. The likelihood of injury and the steps which Sutton might have taken to lessen or eliminate the risk were factors which had to be taken into account. Sutton had admitted that it should have removed the boat and could have avoided the injury to J by so doing. No additional expense would have been incurred. Accordingly, the injury suffered by J was within the reasonably foreseeable category and Sutton was liable.

Unfair Contract Terms Act 1977

At common law, an occupier was entitled to take steps to exclude liability for negligence (e.g. erecting notices disclaiming liability). The 1957 Act did not alter the law in this respect. However, the Unfair Contract Terms Act 1977 severely restricts the ability of an occupier to exclude or limit liability for breach of the common duty of care.

Section 2(1) of the 1977 Act provides that no-one can, by contract or by notice, exclude or restrict their liability for death or personal injury resulting from negligence. In the case of other loss or damage (e.g. to property or goods), liability for negligence can only be excluded if it is reasonable to do so.

It is common for notices to be erected in parks and other recreational areas purporting to relieve the occupier (usually the local authority) from liability for loss or damage to those using the park. Such notices are ineffective to exclude liability for death and personal injury. They may also be ineffective if they seek to exclude liability for damage to property caused by, or as the result of negligence by, the local authority and members of its staff or its agents.

The 1977 Act applies to all local authorities. Section 14 defines 'business' to include 'a profession and the activities of any government department or local or public authority'.

Occupiers' Liability Act 1984

The 1984 Act has two purposes:

(a) to clarify and amend the duty owed by the occupiers (including local authorities) of premises (i.e. land, buildings and other structures both movable and immovable on land) to trespassers and to persons entering land without the consent of the occupier but with lawful authority (e.g. in exercise of a private right of way); and

(b) to amend the Unfair Contract Terms Act 1977 so as to enable an occupier to exclude liability for loss or damage suffered by persons using his premises for recreational or educational activities where these are not business activities of the occupier.

The duty owed by occupiers is set out in section 1(4) of the Act and is to take such action as is reasonable in all circumstances of the case to see that the trespasser or non-visitor does not suffer injury on the premises because of their dangerous state. Section 1(3) of the Act imposes on the occupier of premises the duty if:

(a) he is aware of the danger or has reasonable grounds to believe it exists;

(b) he knows or has reasonable grounds to believe that the trespasser or lawful visitor present without consent is or may be in the vicinity of the danger; and

(c) the risk is one against which, in all the circumstances of the case, he may reasonably be expected to offer some protection.

The duty may be discharged by taking appropriate steps to give warning of the danger and to discourage persons from incurring the risk (e.g. by erecting notices and fencing off the area of land concerned, or both).

No duty is owed by virtue of section 1 of the Act to persons who willingly accept the risk (e.g. those whose hobby it is to explore old mine shafts) or to persons using the highway (normally the highway authority is liable for the dangerous state of the highway).

Section 1A (added by section 13(3) of the Countryside and Rights of Way Act 2000), effectively modifies the duty set out in section 1 in relation to land to which a public right of access exists by virtue of section 2(1) of the 2000 Act. Such land is mountain, moor, heath, down and registered common land as shown on the access maps. In determining whether or not a duty is owed by the occupier by virtue of section 1 of the 1984 Act to such land, regard is to be had in particular to:

(a) the fact that the existence of the right ought not to place an undue burden on the occupant;

(b) the importance of maintaining the character of the countryside, including features of historic, traditional or archaeological interest; and

(c) any relevant guidance given under section 20 of the 2000 Act.

Breach of the duty does not give rise to liability for loss of, or damage to, property.

In relation to the Unfair Contract Terms Act 1977, section 2 of the 1984 Act amends the 1977 Act by altering the definition of business liability so that the owner or occupier of land who runs a business there (e.g. farming or forestry) may exclude liability for death or injury to visitors who are granted free access for recreational or educational purposes. If a charge is made, then the access becomes a business purpose and such liability cannot be excluded. Local authorities are not able to exclude liability to recreational visitors because, as indicated above (section 14 of the 1977 Act), their activities are always treated as business activities.

The leading case in relation to recreation is *Tomlinson v Congleton Borough Council and Others* [2003] UKHL 47. The claimant, T, aged 18, on a hot day went to the park with friends. Ignoring warning signs, he went into the lake, a disused quarry, and dived from a standing position, striking his head. Section 1 of the Occupiers' Liability Act 1984 defined when an occupier owed a duty to persons other than visitors and what the standard of care was. It was essential to use that Act as a template in every case. The claimant accepted that on entering the water he ceased to be a visitor and became a trespasser. The lake, a well-known leisure attraction, was in hot weather a magnet to the public and its sandy beaches an invitation to swim. Unauthorised swimming, the history of accidents and perceived risk of fatality had been acted on by the council over many years. In addition to prominent notices, it employed rangers who gave out oral warnings and safety leaflets, but those warnings were ineffective. In 1990 the council, aware that the beach areas encouraged swimming, had agreed to plant over them. However, that work, begun only shortly before the accident, was incomplete.

The judge at first instance held that the council was not liable, there being no danger in the state of the premises. On appeal, the Court of Appeal, by a majority, reversed the judge's ruling. On further appeal by the council, the House of Lords reversed the Court of Appeal's decision and restored the decision of the judge. The only risk, within the scope of the 1984 Act, arose from what T had chosen to do, not from the state of the premises. He was a person of full age and capacity who had voluntarily, without any pressure or inducement, engaged in an inherently risky activity. The council was not therefore in breach of its obligations under the 1984 Act. It was contrary to common sense to require the occupier of premises to provide protection against an obvious danger on his land arising from a natural feature such as a lake.

Insurance

Any local authority, or other person, who owns or manages parks or open spaces to which the public have access should have adequate public liability insurance to cover claims for damages for death, personal injury and damage to, or loss of, property.

Chapter 7

LICENSING OF EVENTS UNDER THE LICENSING ACT 2003

General

Under the Licensing Act 2003, certain activities, called 'licensable activities', are required to be licensed by a licensing authority. These activities comprise:

(a) the sale by retail of alcohol;

(b) the supply of alcohol by or on behalf of a club to, or to the order of, a member of the club;

(c) the provision of regulated entertainment;

(d) the provision of late night entertainment.

This chapter is concerned only with the provision of regulated entrainment, the other activities being outside the scope of this book.[1]

'The provision of regulated entertainment' is defined in great detail in Part 1 of Schedule 1 to the 2003 Act. Entertainment is defined as:

(a) a performance of a play;

(b) an exhibition of a film;

(c) an indoor sporting event;

(d) a boxing or wrestling entertainment;

---

[1] More extensive coverage of the Licensing Act 2003 can be found in *Alcohol and Entertainment Licensing: A Practical Guide* published by Shaw & Sons.

(e) a performance of live or recorded music;

(f) any playing of recorded music;

(g) a performance of dance;

(h) entertainment of a similar description not falling within (e), (f) or (g).

The entertainment must be in the presence of an audience or spectators and be provided for the purpose, wholly or partly, of entertaining the audience or the spectators. Except in the case of (c), the activity may take place in the open air.

Part 2 of Schedule 1 provides for exemptions from the foregoing definition. These include religious meetings or services, the provision of a film as part of an exhibit in a museum or art gallery, garden fêtes and similar events and entertainment provided in a vehicle in motion. A vehicle is defined in section 193 as a vehicle intended or adapted for use on the roads.

Subject to the exemptions, licensable activities require a licence from the licensing authority to be lawfully carried on. The licensing authorities are:

(a) the council of a district in England;

(b) the council of a county in England in which there are no district councils;

(c) the council of a county or county borough in Wales;

(d) the council of a London borough;

(e) the Common Council of the City of London;

(f) the Sub-Treasurer of the Inner Temple;

(g) the Under-Treasurer of the Middle Temple;

(h) the Council of the Isles of Scilly.

Premises licence

Unless temporary entertainment is being provided (see below, page 111) or the entertainment or location is exempt under Part 2 of Schedule 1 (paragraphs 5 to 12) or sections 173 to 175 of the 2003 Act respectively (see below), a provider of regulated entertainment must obtain a premises licence or club premises certificate from the relevant licensing authority. A premises licence authorises the use of a particular premises for the relevant licensable activities. This does not, however, affect planning or health and safety, etc. requirements; nor does it obviate the need to obtain copyright licences for performances of plays, music or other forms of entertainment from such bodies as the Performing Right Society, the Mechanical-Copyright Protection Society or Phonographic Performance Ltd., or from a copyright owner under copyright legislation.

Fees are normally payable for a premises licence, comprising an initial fee payable on application and an annual fee thereafter. The amount of the fee is based on the value of the premises for non-domestic rating purposes. No fees are payable for a premises licence for a church hall, chapel hall or other similar building, a village hall, or community hall or other similar building (Regulations 9 and 10 of the Licensing Act 2003 (Fees) Regulations 2005 (SI 2005/79)). There is thus no exemption from the payment of fees for a premises licence for regulated entertainment in the open air. However, in its general guidance on the 2003 Act, the DCMS seeks to encourage local authorities to consider seeking premises licences from their licensing authority for public spaces within the community in their own name. This could include village greens, market squares and open spaces. No additional licence would then need to be obtained by anyone else carrying out licensable activities covered by such a licence, although, for privately organised events, the consent of the local authority holding the licence would usually be required and permission given to use the land. The DCMS guidance can be viewed on its website: www.culture.gov.uk.

Exemptions
Part 2 of Schedule 1 to the 2003 Act exempts specified activities from the need to obtain a licence. The exemptions relate to:

(a) films used for advertising, demonstration or education purposes;

(b) films which are exhibits or part of an exhibit at museums and art galleries;

(c) music (live or recorded) which is incidental to (b) or is not the provision of entertainment facilities;

(d) use of television and radio receivers;

(e) the provision of entertainment at religious services or places of public religious worship;

(f) garden fêtes which are not held for the purposes of private gain;

(g) morris dancing and the like or unamplified live music which is an integral part of such dancing;

(h) provision of entertainment in a vehicle in motion which is not permanently or temporarily parked.

Sections 173 and 174 of the 2003 Act exempt licensable

activities from licensing requirements when carried on at various locations, including the following which are relevant to the scope of this book:

(a) a royal palace;

(b) premises occupied by the armed forces of the Crown;

(c) where the Secretary of State has issued a certificate in the interests of national security;

(d) at such other places as may be prescribed (at the time or publication, none of relevance to parks and open spaces had been prescribed).

Section 175 of the 2003 Act (as substituted by the Gambling Act 2005) exempts from the need to have a licence a non-commercial lottery where prizes consist of or include alcohol in a sealed container.

Temporary event notice

Sections 100 to 110 of the 2003 Act make provision for the licensing of temporary events by means of a temporary event notice. Only an individual can give a temporary event notice, so that if an organisation or body (e.g. a local council or a charity) wishes to stage a temporary event, it must appoint an individual to give the notice.

There are limitations on the number of events and the scale of events, as follows:

(a) the number of times a person (the premises user) may give a temporary event notice (50 times per year for a personal licence holder and five times per year for other people);

(b) the number of times a temporary event notice may be given for any particular premises (12 times in a calendar year);

(c) the length of time a temporary event may last (96 hours);

(d) the maximum total duration of the periods covered by temporary event notices at any individual premises (15 days in any 12-month period); and

(e) the scale of the event in terms of the maximum number of people attending at any one time (less than 500).

A personal licence holder is an individual who holds a licence for the supply of alcohol in accordance with a premises licence.

Temporary events do not have to be authorised as such by the licensing authority. Instead, the premises user notifies the event to the licensing authority and the police in the manner prescribed by the Licensing Act 2003 (Permitted Temporary Activities) (Notices) Regulations 2005 (SI 2005/2918). A fee is payable.

Chapter 8

FORESHORE AND SEASHORE

Introduction

Foreshore is that part of the shore between the high and low water marks of ordinary tides. In common parlance, the word seashore has a more extensive meaning and is generally taken to include waste ground above the upper limit of the foreshore. In section 49(1) of the Coast Protection Act 1949, the word 'seashore' means the bed and shore of the sea and of every channel, creek, bay or estuary, and of every river as far up that river as the tide flows, and any cliff, bank, barrier, dune, beach flat or other land adjacent to the shore. However, the Fourth Schedule to the Act excludes specified creeks and river areas from the ambit of the Act.

Prima facie the ownership of the foreshore is in the Crown but quite large stretches are owned by local authorities or leased by them from the Crown. The shore can also be the subject of private ownership with the consequent right to exclude the public therefrom, except for the limited purposes of navigation and fishing.

Some local authorities have owned foreshore rights for centuries whilst others have acquired ownership by virtue of section 164 of the Public Health Act 1875 or private Acts.

The common law rights of the subject

The rights of the subject are rights of navigation and fishing. The owner of the foreshore, if not the Crown, cannot, in respect of his ownership of the soil, make any claim or demand, even if it is expressly granted to him, which in any way interferes with the enjoyment of the public right. Such common law rights, perhaps surprisingly, do not include the right to bathe, although in practice the Crown and other landowners do not usually object to, or take active steps to prevent, bathing.

Extension of the common law rights of the subject

Where a local authority purchases foreshore under the provisions of section 164 of the Public Health Act 1875, it is deemed to be dedicated for the use of the public who can normally bathe there in pursuance of such dedication. Byelaws may be made in regard to bathing, boating and other recreational uses of the seashore. These are dealt with in Chapter 5.

Privately owned foreshore can be made subject to an access order or access agreement under the National Parks and Access to the Countryside Act 1949. Details can be found in *Countryside Law* (see Preface).

Chapter 9

ROYAL PARKS

Introduction

The Royal Parks comprise those parks in London open to the general public and belonging to the Crown. Those which are generally open to the public and are regulated under statutory powers (see below) are:

1. Abingdon Street Garden, being the garden constructed on the sites of properties formerly known as 17–28 (both inclusive) Abingdon Street, London SW1, the garden surrounding the adjoining Jewel Tower, and the lawn surrounding the King George V Memorial.

2. Brompton Cemetery.

3. Bushy Park.

4. The Longford River and those parts of its banks which are for the time being under the control or management of the Secretary of State.

5. Greenwich Park, being those parts of the park which are for the time being under the control or management of the Secretary of State.

6. Grosvenor Square Garden.

7. Hampton Court Gardens.

8. Hampton Court Green.

9. Hampton Court Park.

10. Hyde Park.

115

11. Kensington Gardens.

12. The Natural History Museum Gardens.

13. Primrose Hill.

14. The Regent's Park.

15. Richmond Park.

16. St. James's and The Green Parks.

17. Tower Gardens.

18. Victoria Tower Gardens.

The governing legislation for Royal Parks is the Parks Regulation Act 1872 and the Parks Regulation (Amendment) Act 1926 (itself amended by the Parks Regulation (Amendment) Act 1974). The 1926 Act empowers the Secretary of State to make regulations to be observed by those using the Royal Parks. In exercise of that power, the Secretary of State has made the Royal Parks and Other Open Spaces Regulations 1997 (SI 1997/1639), as amended by the Royal Parks and Other Open Spaces (Amendment) Regulations 2004 (SI 2004/1308).

Regulations

The main provisions of the 1997 Regulations (as amended in 2004) are as follows:

Restriction on use of a Royal Park

Regulation 2 provides that, without the written permission of the Secretary of State, no person:

(a) is allowed to be in a Royal Park when that park is not open to the public;

(b) except in an emergency, may land a helicopter or other aircraft in a Royal Park or enter a park therefrom; or

(c) may permit any animal of which he is in charge to be in any Royal Park in contravention of a notice exhibited by order of the Secretary of State.

Acts prohibited in a Royal Park
Regulation 3 sets out a long list of activities prohibited in Royal Parks. It is not possible to summarise or paraphrase the list in a more readable way than by reproducing the list *verbatim*. The list is prefaced by the words 'Subject to the provisions of Regulation 6, no person using a Park shall' and is as follows:

1. Intentionally or recklessly interfere with the safety, comfort or convenience of any person using a Park in accordance with these Regulations.

2. Deposit waste, litter or any other article into, or do any act which pollutes or is likely to pollute water in, any fountain, lake, pond or river.

3. Drop or leave litter or refuse except in a receptacle provided for the purpose.

4. Unless he is a child of 10 years of age or under, use—

    (a) any pedal cycle, or

    (b) any roller skate, roller blade, skate board or other foot-propelled device

    except on a Park road or in an area designated and marked as being for that purpose by the Secretary of State.

5. Fail to keep any animal of which he is in charge under control or on a lead—

   (a) after having been required by a constable to do so, or

   (b) in contravention of a notice exhibited by order of the Secretary of State.

6. Unless the person is a registered blind person, without reasonable excuse, fail to remove immediately any faeces deposited by any animal of which he is in charge, provided always that it shall not be a reasonable excuse that a person in charge of an animal did not have with him any means of removal of the faeces.

7. Permit any animal of which he is in charge to be tethered or to graze.

8. Fail to remove any animal of which he is in charge from a Park or place in that Park after having been required by a constable to do so.

9. Fail to comply with any direction for the regulation or control of—

   (a) horses or pedal cycles, or

   (b) roller skates, roller blades, skate boards or other foot-propelled devices

   given by a constable or by a notice exhibited by order of the Secretary of State.

10. (a) ride any animal,

    (b) use any pedal cycle, roller skate, roller blade, skate board or other foot-propelled device in any manner that endangers or is likely to endanger any person.

11. (a) use a pedal cycle (other than when it is parked), or

   (b) drive or ride a vehicle

   between sunset and sunrise, or in seriously reduced visibility between sunrise and sunset, unless it is lit in accordance with the Road Vehicles (Lighting) Regulations 1989, and for the purposes of this regulation references in the Road Vehicles (Lighting) Regulations 1989 to a road shall be deemed to be references to a Park road or any other area designated and marked as being an area in which a pedal cycle may be used.

12. Drive or ride any vehicle off a Park road except—

   (a) for the purpose of parking that vehicle in a place reserved for that purpose by the Secretary of State,

   (b) an invalid carriage, or

   (c) a vehicle in use for the purpose of transacting business with any person either residing in a Palace or Park or using land therein under licence from the Secretary of State

   provided in the case of sub-paragraphs (b) and (c) above that the said vehicle is not driven at a speed exceeding 15 mph.

13. In contravention of a notice exhibited by order of the Secretary of State, or after having been required by a constable not to do so—

(a) play any game or engage in any form of sport or exercise,

(b) use any kite or model aircraft or any mechanically propelled or operated model, or

(c) skate or otherwise go on any ice.

14. Fail, when in the public speaking area in Hyde Park, to comply with a direction given by a constable to move from some place in that area or to leave the area.

15. Fail to move any chair, stand or platform in the public speaking area in Hyde Park in accordance with a direction given by a constable.

16. Fail to comply with a reasonable direction given by a constable to leave a Park or any part thereof.

Acts in a Royal Park for which written permission is required

Regulation 4 provides that, unless the Secretary of State's written permission has first been obtained, no person using a Park shall:

1. Interfere with any plant or fungus.

2. Go on any flower bed or shrubbery, or on any area of a Royal Park access to which is prohibited by a notice exhibited by order of the Secretary of State.

3. Use or operate a metal or mineral detector or any device for locating objects below ground level.

4. Attach any article to, climb or interfere with any tree, railing, fence, statue, seat, building or structure.

5. Interfere with any notice or sign.

6. Carry on any trade or business in a Royal Park, offer anything for sale or hire or expose or have in his possession anything for the purpose of sale or hire therein.

7. Use language which publicly intimates that any article, commodity, facility or service can be obtained in a Royal Park or elsewhere.

8. Exhibit any notice or advertisement or any other written or pictorial matter.

9. Play or cause to be played a musical instrument.

10. Use any apparatus for the transmission, reception, reproduction or amplification of sound, speech or images, except apparatus designed and used as an aid to defective hearing, or apparatus used in a vehicle so as not to produce sound audible to a person outside that vehicle, or apparatus used where the sound is received through headphones.

11. Discharge any weapon which is a firearm within the meaning of section 57 of the Firearms Act 1968, or project any missile manually or by artificial means.

12. Camp or erect or cause to be erected any tent or enclosure.

13. Wash or dry any piece of clothing or linen.

14. Collect or solicit money or any other gift.

15. Make or give a public speech or address except in the public speaking area in Hyde Park.

16. Unless for the purpose for which it is provided, interfere with or remove any lifebelt, lifeline or lifesaving aid or fixture.

17. Organise or take part in any assembly, display, performance, representation, parade, procession, review or theatrical event.

18. Take photographs of still or moving subjects for the purpose of or in connection with a business, trade, profession or employment or any activity carried on by a body of persons whether corporate or unincorporate.

19. Intentionally obstruct or otherwise interfere with free passage on any road, riding way or path.

20. Fish, take any egg, or intentionally injure or worry any animal or bird.

21. Cause or permit any animal or bird of which he is in charge to chase, worry or injure any other animal or bird.

22. Boat or bathe or otherwise enter any fountain, lake, pond or river, unless—

    (a) in a place for the time being marked by buoys or other means as appointed for that purpose, and

    (b) in accordance with any direction for the control of such activities given by a constable, or by a notice exhibited by order of the Secretary of State.

23. Sail any model except on Adam's Pond in Richmond Park, on the Heron Pond in Bushy Park, on the Rick Pond in Hampton Court Park, or on the Round Pond in Kensington Gardens.

24. Feed or touch any deer or pelican.

25. Ride any animal except—

(a) in Bushy Park,

(b) on the road between Blackheath Gate and St. Mary's Gate in Greenwich Park,

(c) on the riding ways in Hyde Park or St. James's and The Green Parks,

(d) on the road between Queen's Gate and Coalbrookdale Gate in Kensington Gardens,

(e) on the roads in The Regent's Park, or

(f) in Richmond Park.

26. Cause or permit any animal to be in a place for the time being marked by buoys or other means as reserved for bathing or to be in any boat on any water in a Park.

27. Drive or ride any vehicle which is constructed, adapted or in use for the purpose of a trade or business except as specified in Part I of Schedule 2 to the Regulations (i.e taxis, vehicles being used to transact business with a person residing in a Royal Park or working there, breakdown vehicles attending a breakdown).

28. Drive or ride any vehicle on a Royal Park road in excess of the speed specified in relation to that road in Part II of Schedule 2 to the Regulations (the speed limits vary according to location from 30 mph down to 10 mph).

29. Tow or leave any caravan.

30. Unless in an emergency, cause any vehicle to wait, or leave any vehicle unattended, in a place other than one for the time being appointed for the parking of a vehicle of that description by the Secretary of State.

31. Cause or permit any fire to be lit or to place, throw or let fall a lighted match, similar object or any other thing so as to be likely to cause a fire.

General

Regulation 5 provides that, where a constable has reasonable ground for belief that a person has contravened any one or more of the Regulations, that person shall give on demand his name and address to that constable.

Policing and trading

Policing of the Royal Parks was originally carried out by the Royal Parks Constabulary. The Constabulary was abolished by section 161 of the Serious Organised Crime and Police Act 2005 and, under powers given by section 162 of that Act, responsibility for policing was transferred by the Secretary of State to the Metropolitan Police by the Royal Parks (Regulation of Specified Parks) Order 2005 (SI 2005/1522).

Trading in the Royal Parks is governed by the Royal Parks (Trading) Act 2000. The Act empowers the Secretary of State to designate specific regulations in the 1997 Regulations (see above) as park trading regulations, failure to comply with which is an offence. The Secretary of State has made the Royal Parks and Other Open Spaces (Trading) Regulations 2000 (SI 2000/2949). This designates Regulation 4(6) of the 1997 Regulations as a park trading regulation.

Management

The Royal Parks is an executive agency of the Department for Culture, Media and Sport (DCMS). Its website is www.royalparks.org.uk.

The Royal Parks purpose is 'To manage the Royal Parks effectively and efficiently; balancing the responsibility to conserve and enhance these unique environments with creative policies to encourage access and to increase opportunities for enjoyment, education, entertainment and healthy recreation.'

Chapter 10

SPECIAL PROVISIONS RELATING TO LONDON

Introduction

Outside the City of London, the present structure of London government was largely enacted by the London Government Act 1963, which created the London boroughs, and the Greater London Authority Act 1999, which created the Greater London Authority and the office of Mayor of London. The City of London is primarily governed by its own legislation but many Acts have been applied to the City, including Acts relating to parks and open spaces.

Section 58(1) of the 1963 Act applies the Open Spaces Act 1906 (except section 14 – power of county councils to provide public walks and pleasure grounds) to the London boroughs. Section 1 of the 1906 Act includes the Common Council of the City of London as a local authority for the purposes of the Act. The 1906 Act is covered in Chapter 4.

Section 40 of the 1963 Act generally applies the provisions of the Public Health Acts 1875–1925, 1936 and 1961 to the London boroughs. In addition, section 180(1) of the Local Government Act 1972 provides that local authorities, for the purposes of these Acts, include the London boroughs, the Common Council of the City of London and the respective treasurers of the Inner and Middle Temples.

Management of open spaces

The open spaces held or managed by the London borough councils are managed under the Ministry of Housing and Local Government Provisional Order Confirmation (Greater London Parks and Open Spaces) Act 1967. The main detailed provisions are set out in Part II of the Schedule to the Act and are as follows. Sections refer to the sections in Part II of the Schedule.

Facilities for public recreation

Section 7(1) empowers a London borough council to provide and maintain:

(a) swimming baths and bathing places whether open air or indoor;

(b) golf courses and grounds, tracks, lawns, courts, greens and such other open air facilities as the council thinks fit for any form of recreation whatsoever;

(c) gymnasia;

(d) rifle ranges;

(e) indoor facilities for any form of recreation whatsoever;

(f) centres and other facilities (whether indoor or open air) for the use of clubs, societies or organisations whose objects or activities are wholly or mainly of a recreational, social or educational character;

(g) amusement fairs and entertainments including bands of music, concerts, dramatic performances, cinematograph exhibitions and pageants (but the area set aside for spectators must not exceed one acre or one-tenth of the open space, whichever is the greater);

(h) exhibitions and trade fairs for the purpose of promoting education, the conservation of the environment, recreation, industry, commerce, crafts or the arts (but not on more than eight Sundays in any year);

(i)   in time of frost facilities for skating, and flood any part of the open space in order to provide ice for skating;

(j)   meals and refreshments of all kinds to sell to the public;

(k) swings, platforms, screens, chairs, seats, lockers, towels, costumes and any apparatus, appliances, equipment or conveniences necessary or desirable for persons resorting to the open space;

(l)   such buildings or structures as the council considers necessary or desirable including (without prejudice to the generality of this paragraph) buildings for the accommodation of keepers and other persons employed in connection with the open space.

Section 7(1) also empowers a council to set apart or enclose in connection with any of the foregoing any part of the open space and preclude any person from entering that part so set apart or enclosed other than a person to whom access is permitted by the council or (where the right of so setting apart or enclosing is granted to any person by the council under the powers of the 1967 Order) by such person.

Restrictions
However, section 7(1) also sets out various provisos restricting the foregoing powers as follows:

(a) where a part of an open space set apart or enclosed for the playing of games under the above provision is not laid out and maintained for that purpose then, while the part is not in actual use for games, persons cannot be precluded from entering therein;

(b) any part of an open space set apart or enclosed for the use of persons listening to or viewing an entertainment shall not exceed one acre or one-tenth of the open space, whichever is the greater;

(c) where any entertainment is provided in an open space, there are restrictions on the type of cinematograph film to be exhibited in any building, on the charges for admission thereto, on the terms of a grant or letting of the use of the building for the purpose of a cinematograph entertainment and on the provision by a local authority of a cinematograph exhibition on Sundays in an open space outside Greater London.

Licences to provide facilities and letting of land and buildings for public recreation

By section 8 of Part II of the Schedule to the 1967 Act, a council may grant to any person the right of exercising any of the powers conferred upon the local authority by section 7 and, for those purposes, may let to any person any building or structure and any part of an open space set apart or enclosed. The section also empowers a council to contribute towards the expenses to be incurred by any person in the provision of any entertainment or otherwise in pursuance of any such grant or letting.

Restriction of public rights

Section 9 provides that a council may enclose during such periods and subject to such conditions as it considers necessary or expedient any part of any open space for the purpose of, or in connection with, the cultivation or preservation of vegetation in the interest of public amenity, or in the interest of the safety of the public, and may preclude any person from entering any part so enclosed.

Charges

Section 10(a) empowers a council to make such reasonable charges as it thinks fit for the use or enjoyment of anything provided by them under items (a) to (l) above.

Section 10(b) authorises any person to whom any right is granted or any building or structure is let under section 8 to make reasonable charges in respect of the purposes for which the council itself may make charges under section 10(a).

Restrictions on powers under sections 7 to 10

The powers given by sections 7 to 10 may not be exercised (a) so as to contravene any private rights which a person may have otherwise than as a member of the public (e.g. a private right of access to a house); and (b) without the consent of a person who is protected by an enactment or scheme, even if that person is under a disability. This could happen where a person is detained under the Mental Health Acts and any consent has to be given by that person's trustee or guardian.

Transfer of open spaces between councils

Section 14 enables a council to transfer the maintenance and management of any open space to another council if they agree that these functions could more conveniently be exercised by the other.

Power to exchange parts of open space for adjoining land

Section 15 provides that, for the purpose of enlarging or improving any open space, a council may enter into an agreement with the owner of adjacent land for exchanging such land for open space land and the council may pay or receive any moneys for equality of exchange. The council must make full compensation to all parties interested in respect of any private rights extinguished under or by virtue of the section and such compensation must be settled in the manner provided by the Land Compensation Act 1961.

Powers for private owners of land
Section 16 of Part II of the Schedule to the 1967 Act permits owners of land to grant rights of pre-emption to a council for the purpose of providing an open space or for the purposes of the Physical Training and Recreation Act 1937. However, these powers shall not be exercised in respect of land outside Greater London except with the consent of the council of the county in which the land is situate.

The provisions of the 1937 Act relating to recreation have been repealed. Presumably, therefore, the specific powers of pre-emption in section 16 are no longer exercisable. The powers of local authorities generally formerly contained in the 1937 Act have been effectively replaced by section 19 of the Local Government (Miscellaneous Provisions) Act 1976 (see Chapter 4), but this section contains no saving for section 16 of the 1967 Order.

Use of portions of open spaces for street improvements
Section 17 empowers a council, with the consent of the Secretary of State, to utilise, alienate or exchange for other land any part of any open space for the purpose of the construction, widening or alteration of any street. The council has to fix on, or in the vicinity of, the open space a placard giving specified particulars and the Secretary has to consider any representations as to the proposal before giving his consent.

Any land acquired under this section by a council in exchange for an open space otherwise than for addition to an existing open space shall be deemed to have been acquired under the Open Spaces Act 1906 (see Chapters 2 and 4).

Park officers and constables

Section 18 provides that a council may procure officers appointed by it for securing the observance of the provisions of all enactments relating to open spaces under their control or management and of the byelaws and regulations made thereunder to be sworn in as constables for that purpose but any such officer shall not act as a constable unless in uniform or provided with a warrant.

Section 19 provides that any constable or officer of a council authorised in writing to enforce byelaws having effect in relation to an open space may, without other warrant than this order, seize and detain any person committing or having committed any offence against such byelaws.

Powers are additional

Section 20 provides that the powers conferred upon a council by or in pursuance of Part II of the Schedule to the Act are in addition to and not in derogation of any other powers possessed by the council independently of the Act.

Greater London squares and gardens

Some squares and gardens in Greater London are held by trustees, some by private householders and some by local authorities. A number of them are regulated by special Acts and full information regarding them is to be found in the Report of the Royal Commission on London Squares (Cmd. 3196 of 1928).

In particular, reference should be made of the London Squares Preservation Act 1931 (private). This Act ensures that the squares to which it refers are used only for authorised purposes and that alternative open spaces are to be provided to the satisfaction of the Greater London Council if any estates containing any of the squares are redeveloped. Certain functions exercisable by the former London County Council under this Act are now exercisable by the inner London boroughs and by the Common Council of the City of London (see the Local Law (Greater London Council and Inner London Boroughs) Order 1965 (SI 1965/540, as amended by SI 1966/1250)).

Grosvenor Square has been excluded from the provisions of the 1931 Act and has been laid out as a garden for the exercise and enjoyment of the public.

The Town Gardens Protection Act 1863 (see Chapters 2 and 4) also applies to enclosed gardens and ornamental grounds in Greater London.

City of London Corporation

The City of London owns and manages parks and open spaces outside the boundaries of the City. The most notable is Hampstead Heath which was transferred to the City by the London Government Reorganisation (Hampstead Heath) Order 1989 (SI 1989/304). The City has the powers of management set out in Part II of the Schedule to the 1967 Act mentioned above.

Under the Corporation of London (Open Spaces) Act 1878 (private), the City was empowered to acquire common or commonable land and open space within 25 miles from the City boundary. Using these powers, the City has acquired Burnham Beeches in Buckinghamshire and Farthing Down and Coulsdon Common in the London Borough of Croydon.

The Metropolitan Public Gardens Association

The Metropolitan Public Gardens Association is a registered charity. It was established in 1882 with the principal object being 'the protection, preservation, safeguarding and acquiring for permanent preservation for public use, of gardens, disused burial grounds, churchyards, open spaces, areas of land likely to be used for building purposes, strips of land adjoining roads and footpaths, or any land situated within the Metropolitan Police District or in its vicinity'. An additional object was, and still is, the provision of seats and the planting of trees.

The Association provides modest grants to those who share a desire to improve the environment and quality of life for the local community.

The Association's website is www.mpga.org.uk.

APPENDICES – MODEL BYELAWS

GUIDANCE NOTES: ARRANGEMENTS FOR CONFIRMATION OF LOCAL AUTHORITY BYELAWS

Following the general election on 7 June 2001, responsibility for the confirmation of certain byelaws was transferred from the Home Secretary to the Secretary of State for Transport, Local Government and the Regions. These responsibilities were later transferred to the Office of the Deputy Prime Minister in May 2002, and subsequently Communities and Local Government in May 2006.

About this guidance

This Guidance page (updated May 2007) replaces the Home Office Circular 25/1996: Arrangements for Confirmation of Local Authority Byelaws, and sets out the arrangements for the processing of those byelaws for which the Secretary of State for Communities and Local Government is the confirming authority.

Deciding how to apply to have byelaws confirmed

1. A byelaw is a local law which is made by a statutory body, such as a local authority, under an enabling power established by an Act of Parliament. If there is general legislation to cover the subject causing concern, byelaws are not generally considered suitable. Since byelaws create criminal offences, they cannot come into effect unless they have been confirmed by a Secretary of State.

2. The chart at Annex 1 *(not reproduced)* sets out the procedure for establishing whether byelaws

   - are likely to be appropriate, and

   - are ones for which the Secretary of State is the confirming authority.

3. Communities and Local Government currently has seven sets of model byelaws which set out an appropriate wording

for byelaws on a number of different subjects. We may add to or amend these in the light of experience, demand and changing circumstances.

4. Councils should note that, in a number of the sets, some of the individual model byelaws are optional and only those which are needed should be adopted. For example, if making byelaws using model set 2 (Pleasure Grounds, Public Walks and Open Spaces), do not include byelaws to restrict horses if there is no experience of them ever entering the park, nor restrict fishing if there is no water.

5. Once a Council has established that the issue to be addressed is dealt with by a model, the Council should locate a copy of the relevant set from the local government section of the Communities and Local Government website at www.communities.gov.uk/index.asp?id=1133678, and adapt it according to their needs using the guidance notes that accompany the set.

6. Care should be taken to ensure that no changes are made to the wording of the model byelaws to be adopted. Where a Council wishes to vary a model or to make byelaws on an issue not covered by an available model, Part B of the application for provisional approval should also be completed.

7. In all cases, the draft byelaws and the completed application form for provisional approval should be submitted together to the Communities and Local Government Byelaws Section. Only when provisional approval has been given should the Council make, seal and advertise the byelaws.

8. Councils should also note that where there is a substantive error in byelaws that have been sealed and advertised, the byelaws cannot simply be amended either by the Council or by Communities and Local Government. They must be made, sealed and advertised again. It is therefore important that the byelaws are checked in detail before sealing. (Very minor typographical errors may, however, be corrected by a Council officer if the corrections carry a clear official mark.)

Purpose of an application form

9. The proforma application for provisional approval, which must be completed in respect of every byelaw application, serves two purposes.

10. The first is to assist Councils by providing them with an aide memoire of the issues that need to be addressed. The second is to help Communities and Local Government by providing confirmation that attention has been given to those issues.

Level of scrutiny by Communities and Local Government

11. As a general principle, it is for the local authority to decide the necessary and appropriate byelaws for its area. Provided there is no legal problem and no conflict with general Government policy, we shall not oppose or query a byelaw simply because our judgement of what is necessary or appropriate differs from the Council's. Nor shall we oppose or query aspects of byelaws which relate to purely local concerns, such as the precise areas to which they will apply.

12. We shall assume that the wording of any byelaws has been checked and is deliberate: this assumption will apply to any omissions or inclusions and any statement of areas to which the byelaws will extend. Unless an apparent error has legal implications or affects a point of principle, we shall not take it up with the Council.

13. We shall continue to expect Councils to consult with any interested parties and address their concerns as far as possible. Any objections we receive, as a result of the advertisement of the byelaws, will be sent to the Council for its comments.

14. We shall also continue to expect that byelaws are certain in their terms and not unreasonable in the legal sense. Only the courts, however, can give a definitive ruling. We shall therefore, not enter into discussions of these issues in particular cases but raise with Councils only those byelaws which clearly fail to meet the requirements.

15. In considering an application, the points on which Communities and Local Government will concentrate are as follows:

   - that the byelaws are *intra vires* the relevant legislation and that any action required by the legislation, such as consultation with a named public body, has been taken;

   - that they do not duplicate or conflict with the general law, existing byelaws or any local Act, or common law;

   - that the nuisance they address merits criminal sanctions and that, to a reasonable person, the penalty available is proportionate;

   - that they directly address a genuine and specific local problem and do not attempt to deal in general terms with essentially national issues;

   - that they do not conflict with Government policy.

16. Byelaws which exactly follow a model will in most cases meet these criteria. For other byelaws, we will look to Councils to provide answers on these points.

Making the byelaws

17. **When the council has formally resolved to adopt any byelaws, they should be made under the common seal of the authority and should be placed after any schedule or plan included in the byelaws. The document should also be signed and dated.**

18. Where the byelaws are made by a parish or community council not having a seal, they should be made under the hands and seals of two members of the council. In this case, a suitable subscription to the byelaws would be:

   Given under our hands and seals this .... day of ....

   (Signed) .... (Seal)

   (Signed) .... (Seal)

   Members of the .... Parish/Town Council.

19. If members of the parish or town council who sign the byelaws do not possess personal seals, the imprint of a signet ring, coin or thumb will suffice. Sealing wax and parchment seals may be obtained from legal stationers.

20. **In order to provide sufficient room for the official signature of the Secretary of State, at least 15 centimetres (6 inches) of space should be left after the council's seal.**

Advertising the byelaws and holding them on deposit

21. After the byelaws have been sealed, a notice of the council's intention to apply for their confirmation must be given in one or more newspapers circulating in the area to which the byelaws are to apply.

22. The usual wording for the newspaper notice is shown below.

COUNTY/DISTRICT/PARISH/TOWN OF ....
CONFIRMATION OF BYELAWS

Notice is hereby given that the County/District/Parish/ Town Council of .... intends after the expiry of the period mentioned below to apply to the Secretary of State for confirmation of byelaws made by the Council [insert here a brief description of the byelaws].

Copies of the byelaws will be kept at the offices of the Council at .... and will be open to inspection without payment on any weekday during the usual office hours for one calendar month from and after the date of the [first] publication of this notice. Copies of the byelaws will also be supplied on receipt of an application accompanied by a fee of .... for each copy.

Any objection to the application for the confirmation of the byelaws may be made by letter addressed to Communities and Local Government Byelaws Section, 5/G10 Eland House, Bressenden Place, London SW1E 5DU (no later than one week after the closing date for inspection) before the byelaws are confirmed.

(Signed) .... Proper Officer of the Council

(Dated) ....

23. For at least one month after the date of the publication of the newspaper(s), a **copy** of the byelaws must be held on deposit at the offices of the council for inspection by the public at all reasonable hours.

24. The period of deposit cannot begin until the byelaws have been brought into existence by being sealed. To avoid confusion, councils are advised to ensure that the byelaws are advertised **after** they have been sealed.

25. The council must provide any person who applies with a copy of the byelaws or with a copy of any part of the byelaws. A fee of not more than 10 pence should be charged for every 100 words contained in any copy supplied.

Applying for confirmation of the byelaws

26. Application to Communities and Local Government for confirmation should not be made until the month of deposit has expired. The application and sealed byelaws in duplicate (or in triplicate in the case of byelaws for the seashore requiring the consent of the Secretary of State for Transport) should be sent to Communities and Local Government, Byelaws Section, 5/G10 Eland House, Bressenden Place, London SW1E 5DU.

27. The application should state that a copy of the sealed byelaws as forwarded, has been deposited for inspection for a full calendar month since publication of the newspaper(s). A copy of the newspaper(s) or a photocopy of the full page advertising the byelaw should also be enclosed.

28. On receipt of the sealed byelaws, provided that no objections have been received, they will normally be confirmed and returned to you as soon as possible. Where objections have been received, copies may be forwarded to you for the council's comments before a decision is taken.

29. In contentious cases, particularly those where the arguments are finely balanced, it is open to the Secretary of State to order a public inquiry to be held. Such inquiries are rare and,

in the normal course, the Secretary of State would hope that the issues – and any scope for compromise – might be determined locally between the council and objectors.

Date of operation of the byelaws

30. When he confirms byelaws, the Secretary of State may fix the date upon which they are to come into force. The date will normally be one month from the point of confirmation, unless there are special circumstances which make an earlier date desirable. If this is the case, a request and reasons should accompany your application.

Further information

31. Sealed byelaws or any queries on this guidance should be sent by post to the Byelaws Section, 5/G10 Eland House, Bressenden Place, London SW1E 5DU or any other byelaws related matter should be sent by email to byelaws@ communities.gsi.gov.uk.

COUNCILS SHOULD DOWNLOAD THIS SET FROM THE DCLG WEBSITE AND ADAPT IT AS REQUIRED

The guidance notes for Model Byelaws Set 2 should be consulted when using these Model Byelaws.

MODEL BYELAWS – SET 2

[Name of Council]

BYELAWS FOR PLEASURE GROUNDS, PUBLIC WALKS AND OPEN SPACES

ARRANGEMENT OF BYELAWS

PART [1]

GENERAL

1. General interpretation
2. [Application]
3. [Application]
4. Opening times

PART [2]

PROTECTION OF THE GROUND, ITS WILDLIFE AND THE PUBLIC

5. Protection of structures and plants
6. Unauthorised erection of structures
7. Climbing
8. Grazing
9. Protection of wildlife
10. Gates
11. Camping
12. Fires
13. Missiles
14. Interference with life-saving equipment

PART [5]
WATERWAYS

PART [6]
MODEL AIRCRAFT

PART [7]
OTHER REGULATED ACTIVITIES

PART [8]
MISCELLANEOUS

Byelaws made under [section 164 of the Public Health Act 1875/section 15 of the Open Spaces Act 1906/sections 12 and 15 of the Open Spaces Act 1906] by the *insert name of Council* with respect to *insert name of ground/description of its location/* [pleasure grounds, public walks and open spaces].

[PART 1]
GENERAL

General interpretation

1. In these byelaws:

Select from the following list only terms to be used in the byelaws which the Council proposes to adopt:

"the Council" means *insert name of Council;*

"the ground" means *insert name of ground or a description of its location/*[any of the grounds listed in [the Schedule /Schedule [1]];

"designated area" means an area in the ground which is set aside for a specified purpose, that area and its purpose to be indicated by notices placed in a conspicuous position;

"invalid carriage" means a vehicle, whether mechanically propelled or not,

(a) the unladen weight of which does not exceed 150 kilograms,

(b) the width of which does not exceed 0.85 metres, and

(c) which has been constructed or adapted for use for the carriage of a person suffering from a disability, and used solely by such a person.

Application

Councils should adopt EITHER model byelaw 2 or model byelaw 3

2. These byelaws apply to *insert name of ground or a description of its location/* [all of the grounds listed in [the Schedule/ Schedule 1].

3. These byelaws apply to all of the grounds listed in [the Schedule/Schedule 1] unless otherwise stated.

Opening times

4. (1) No person shall enter or remain in the ground except during opening hours.

Where byelaw is to apply to more than one ground

    (2) "Opening hours" means the days and times during which the ground is open to the public and which are indicated by a notice placed in a conspicuous position at the entrance to the ground.

Where byelaw is to apply to more than one ground

    (3) Byelaw [4(1)] applies only to the grounds listed in [Part 1 of] Schedule [2].]

PART [2]
PROTECTION OF THE GROUND, ITS WILDLIFE AND THE PUBLIC

Protection of structures and plants

5. (1) No person shall without reasonable excuse remove from or displace within the ground:

    (a) any barrier, post, seat or implement, or any part of a structure or ornament provided for use in the laying out or maintenance of the ground; or

    (b) any stone, soil or turf or the whole or any part of any plant, shrub or tree.

    (2) No person shall walk on or ride, drive or station a horse or any vehicle over:

    (a) any flower bed, shrub or plant;

    (b) any ground in the course of preparation as a flower bed or for the growth of any tree, shrub or plant; or

    (c) any part of the ground set aside by the Council for the renovation of turf or for other landscaping purposes and indicated by a notice conspicuously displayed.

Unauthorised erection of structures

6. No person shall without the consent of the Council erect any barrier, post, ride or swing, building or any other structure.

Climbing

7. No person shall without reasonable excuse climb any wall or fence in or enclosing the ground, or any tree, or any barrier, railing, post or other structure.

Grazing

8. No person shall without the consent of the Council turn out or permit any animal for which he is responsible to graze in the ground.

Protection of wildlife

9. No person shall kill, injure, take or disturb any animal, or engage in hunting or shooting or the setting of traps or the laying of snares.

Gates

10. (1) No person shall leave open any gate to which this byelaw applies and which he has opened or caused to be opened.

    (2) Byelaw 10(1) applies to any gate to which is attached, or near to which is displayed, a conspicuous notice stating that leaving the gate open is prohibited.

Camping

11. No person shall without the consent of the Council erect a tent or use a vehicle, caravan or any other structure for the purpose of camping [except in a designated area for camping].

Fires

12. (1) No person shall light a fire or place, throw or drop a lighted match or any other thing likely to cause a fire.

(2) Byelaw 12(1) shall not apply to:

[(a)] [the lighting of a fire at any event for which the Council has given permission that fires may be lit;][or]

[(b)] [the lighting or use, in such a manner as to safeguard against damage or danger to any person, of a properly constructed camping stove, in a designated area for camping, or of a properly constructed barbecue, in a designated area for barbecues].

Missiles

13. No person shall throw or use any device to propel or discharge in the ground any object which is liable to cause injury to any other person.

Interference with life-saving equipment

14. No person shall except in case of emergency remove from or displace within the ground or otherwise tamper with any life-saving appliance provided by the Council.

PART [3]
HORSES, CYCLES AND VEHICLES

Interpretation of Part [3]

15. In this Part:

"designated route" means a route in or through the ground which is set aside for a specified purpose, its route and that purpose to be indicated by notices placed in a conspicuous position;

"motor cycle" means a mechanically-propelled vehicle, not being an invalid carriage, with less than four wheels and the weight of which does not exceed 410 kilograms;

"motor vehicle" means any mechanically-propelled vehicle other than a motor cycle or an invalid carriage;

"trailer" means a vehicle drawn by a motor vehicle and includes a caravan.

154

Horses

Horse riding permitted

16. No person shall ride a horse in the ground in such a manner as to cause danger to any other person.

Horse riding prohibited except in certain grounds (subject to bridleway, etc)

17. (1) No person shall ride a horse except:

> (a) in any of the grounds listed in Part [3] of Schedule [2]; or

> (b) in the exercise of a lawful right or privilege.

(2) Where horse riding is permitted in any ground by virtue of byelaw [17](1)(a) or a lawful right or privilege, no person shall ride a horse in such a manner as to cause danger to any other person.

Horse riding prohibited (subject to bridleway, etc)

18. (1) No person shall ride a horse except in the exercise of a lawful right or privilege.

(2) Where horse riding is permitted by virtue of a lawful right or privilege, no person shall ride a horse in such a manner as to cause danger to any other person.

Horse riding prohibited except on designated route (subject to bridleway, etc)

19. (1) No person shall ride a horse except:

> (a) on a designated route for riding; or

> (b) in the exercise of a lawful right or privilege.

(2) Where horse riding is permitted by virtue of byelaw [19](1)(a) or a lawful right or privilege, no person shall ride a horse in such a manner as to cause danger to any other person.

Cycling

20. No person shall without reasonable excuse ride a cycle in the ground except in any part of the ground where there

is a right of way for cycles [or on a designated route for cycling].

Motor vehicles

21. (1) No person shall without reasonable excuse bring into or drive in the ground a motor cycle, motor vehicle or trailer except in any part of the ground where there is a right of way [or a designated route] for that class of vehicle.

(2) [Where there is a designated route for motor cycles, motor vehicles or trailers, it shall not be an offence under this byelaw to bring into or drive in the ground a vehicle of that class for the sole purpose of transporting it to the route].

Overnight parking

22. No person shall without the consent of the Council leave or cause or permit to be left any motor vehicle in the ground between the hours of 10 p.m. and 6 a.m.

PART [4]
PLAY AREAS, GAMES AND SPORTS

Interpretation of Part [4]

23. In this Part:

"ball games" means any game involving throwing, catching, kicking, batting or running with any ball or other object designed for throwing and catching, but does not include cricket;

"golf course" means any area within the ground set aside for the purposes of playing golf and includes any golf driving range, golf practice area or putting course;

"self-propelled vehicle" means a vehicle other than a cycle, invalid carriage or pram which is propelled by the weight or force of one or more persons skating, sliding or riding on the vehicle or by one or more persons pulling or pushing the vehicle.

Children's play areas

24. No person aged 14 years or over shall enter or remain in a designated area which is a children's play area unless in charge of a child under the age of 14 years.

Children's play apparatus

25. No person aged 14 years or over shall use any apparatus stated to be for the exclusive use of persons under the age of 14 years by a notice conspicuously displayed on or near the apparatus.

Skateboarding, etc

Skateboarding, etc permitted but must not cause danger or annoyance

26. No person shall skate, slide or ride on rollers, skateboards or other self-propelled vehicles in such a manner as to cause danger or give reasonable grounds for annoyance to other persons.

Skateboarding, etc permitted only in designated area

27. (1) No person shall skate, slide or ride on rollers, skateboards or other self-propelled vehicles except in a designated area for such activities.

    (2) Where there is a designated area for skating, sliding or riding on rollers, skateboards or other self-propelled vehicles, no person shall engage in those activities in such a manner as to cause danger or give reasonable grounds for annoyance to other persons.

Ball games

Prohibition of ball games

28. No person shall play ball games in the ground.

Ball games permitted only in designated areas

29. No person shall play ball games in the ground except in a designated area for playing ball games.

Ball games permitted throughout the ground but designated area for ball games also provided

30. No person shall play ball games outside a designated area for playing ball games in such a manner:

   (a) as to exclude persons not playing ball games from use of that part;

   (b) as to cause danger or give reasonable grounds for annoyance to any other person in the ground; or

   (c) which is likely to cause damage to any tree, shrub or plant in the ground.

Rules (to be used with model byelaw 29 or 30)

31. It is an offence for any person using a designated area for playing ball games to break any of the rules set out in Schedule [3] and conspicuously displayed on a sign in the designated area when asked by any person to desist from breaking those rules.

Cricket

32. No person shall throw or strike a cricket ball with a bat except in a designated area for playing cricket.

Archery

33. No person shall engage in the sport of archery except in connection with an event organised by or held with the consent of the Council.

Field sports

34. No person shall throw or put any javelin, hammer, discus or shot except in connection with an event organised by or held with the consent of the Council [or on land set aside by the Council for that purpose].

Golf

Golf prohibited [except where part of ground is set aside as golf course]

35. No person shall drive, chip or pitch a hard golf ball [except on the golf course].

Where part of ground is set aside as a golf course

36. (1) No person shall play golf on the golf course unless he holds a valid ticket issued by or on behalf of the Council entitling him to do so, which ticket shall be retained and shown on demand to any authorised officer or agent of the Council.

(2) No person shall enter on to or remain on the golf course unless:

(a) taking part in the game of golf or accompanying a person so engaged; or

(b) doing so in the exercise of a lawful right or privilege.

(3) No person shall offer his service for hire as an instructor on the golf course without the consent of the Council.

PART [5]
WATERWAYS

Interpretation of Part [5]

37. In this Part:

"boat" means any yacht, motor boat or similar craft but not a model or toy boat;

"power-driven" means driven by the combustion of petrol vapour or other combustible substances;

"waterway" means any river, lake, pool or other body of water and includes any fountain.

Bathing

38. No person shall without reasonable excuse bathe or swim in any waterway [except in a designated area for bathing and swimming].

Ice skating

39. No person shall step onto or otherwise place their weight upon any frozen waterway.

Model boats

40. No person shall operate a power-driven model boat on any
waterway [except in a designated area for model boats].

Boats

*To prohibit use of boats [and if appropriate a wider category of
vessels] without permission [except in designated areas]*

41. No person shall sail or operate any boat, [dinghy, canoe,
sailboard or inflatable] on any waterway without the consent
of the Council [except in a designated area for the sailing or
operation of boats].

In areas where use of boats is common

42. (1) No person shall on any waterway sail or operate any boat
which is not registered with the Council.

(2) A boat is registered for the purposes of byelaw 42(1)
when the owner has made a written application to the
Council and the Council has:

(a) entered the name and address of the owner, a general
description of the boat and the serial number of the
registration in a register kept by an authorised officer
of the Council; and

(b) issued to the owner a certificate of registration
incorporating these particulars.

Fishing

43. No person shall in any waterway cast a net or line for
the purpose of catching fish or other animals [except in a
designated area for fishing].

Pollution

44. No person shall foul or pollute any waterway.

Blocking of watercourses

45. No person shall cause or permit the flow of any drain or watercourse in the ground to be obstructed, diverted, open or shut
or otherwise move or operate any sluice or similar apparatus.

PART [6]
MODEL AIRCRAFT

Interpretation of Part [6]

46. In this Part:

"model aircraft" means an aircraft which weighs not more than 7 kilograms without its fuel;

"power-driven" means driven by:

(a) the combustion of petrol vapour or other combustible substances;

(b) jet propulsion or by means of a rocket, other than by means of a small reaction motor powered by a solid fuel pellet not exceeding 2.54 centimetres in length; or

(c) one or more electric motors or by compressed gas.

"radio control" means control by a radio signal from a wireless transmitter or similar device.

General prohibition

47. No person shall cause any power-driven model aircraft to:

(a) take off or otherwise be released for flight or control the flight of such an aircraft in the ground; or

(b) land in the ground without reasonable excuse.

Model aircraft permitted in certain grounds [on specified days at specified times]

48. Byelaw 47 does not apply to the grounds listed in [Part [5] of Schedule 2] /[column 1 of the table in Part [6] of Schedule [2] on the days and times indicated for each ground in column 2 of that table].

Model aircraft permitted in designated areas

49. No person shall cause any power-driven model aircraft to:

(a) take off or otherwise be released for flight or control the flight of such an aircraft; or

161

(b) land in the ground without reasonable excuse;

other than in a designated area for flying model aircraft.

Model aircraft subject to certain control

50. Byelaw [47]/[49] does not apply to any model aircraft which is [attached to a control line]/[kept under effective radio control].

Quieter types of model aircraft permitted

51. Byelaw [47]/[49] does not apply to any model aircraft which:

(a) gives a noise measurement of not more than 82 dB(A) when measured at a distance of 7 metres from the aircraft in accordance with the Code of Practice issued under the Control of Noise (Code of Practice on Noise from Model Aircraft) Order 1981; and

(b) where it is reasonably practicable to fit, fitted with an effectual silencer or similar device.

PART [7]
OTHER REGULATED ACTIVITIES

Provision of services

52. No person shall without the consent of the Council provide or offer to provide any service for which a charge is made.

Excessive noise

53. (1) No person shall, after being requested to desist by any other person in the ground, make or permit to be made any noise which is so loud or so continuous or repeated as to give reasonable cause for annoyance to other persons in the ground by:

(a) shouting or singing;

(b) playing on a musical instrument; or

(c) by operating or permitting to be operated any radio, amplifier, tape recorder or similar device.

(2) Byelaw 53(1) does not apply to any person holding or taking part in any entertainment held with the consent of the Council.

Public shows and performances

54. No person shall without the consent of the Council hold or take part in any public show or performance.

Aircraft, hang gliders and hot air balloons

55. No person shall except in case of emergency or with the consent of the Council take off from or land in the ground in an aircraft, helicopter, hang glider or hot air balloon.

Kites

56. No person shall fly any kite in such a manner as to cause danger or give reasonable grounds for annoyance to any other person.

Metal detectors

57. (1) No person shall without the consent of the Council use any device designed or adapted for detecting or locating any metal or mineral in the ground.

(2) Byelaw 57(1) shall not apply to *[insert name or description of land]*.

PART [8]
MISCELLANEOUS

Obstruction

58. No person shall obstruct:

(a) any officer of the Council in the proper execution of his duties;

(b) any person carrying out an act which is necessary to the proper execution of any contract with the Council; or

(c) any other person in the proper use of the ground.

Savings

59. (1) It shall not be an offence under these byelaws for an officer of the Council or any person acting in accordance with a contract with the Council to do anything necessary to the proper execution of his duty.

    (2) Nothing in or done under these byelaws shall in any respect prejudice or injuriously affect any public right of way through the ground, or the rights of any person acting lawfully by virtue of some estate, right or interest in, over or affecting the ground or any part of the ground.

Removal of offenders

60. Any person offending against any of these byelaws may be removed from the ground by an officer of the Council or a constable.

Penalty

61. Any person offending against any of these byelaws shall be liable on summary conviction to a fine not exceeding level 2 on the standard scale.

Revocation

62. The byelaws made by *insert name* on *insert date* and confirmed by *insert name of confirming authority* on *insert date of confirmation* relating to the ground are hereby revoked.

Limited revocation to preserve byelaws relating to dogs

63. Byelaws *insert numbers of byelaws being revoked* made by *insert name* on *insert date* and confirmed by *insert name of confirming authority* on *insert date of confirmation* relating to the ground are hereby revoked.

SCHEDULES

SCHEDULE [1]
GROUNDS TO WHICH BYELAWS APPLY [GENERALLY]

The grounds referred to in byelaw [2]/[3] are:

...

SCHEDULE [2]
GROUNDS REFERRED TO IN CERTAIN BYELAWS
PART [1]
OPENING TIMES (BYELAW [4](1))

...

PART [2]
HORSE RIDING PROHIBITED EXCEPT IN CERTAIN GROUNDS (SUBJECT TO BRIDLEWAY, ETC) (BYELAW [17](1))

...

PART [3]
USE OF MODEL AIRCRAFT PERMITTED ON SPECIFIED DAYS AT SPECIFIED TIMES (BYELAW [48])

Name or description of ground	Days and times at which use of model aircraft is permitted
Park E	
Park F	

SCHEDULE [3]
RULES FOR PLAYING BALL GAMES IN DESIGNATED AREAS (BYELAW [31])

Any person using a designated area for playing ball games is required by byelaw [31] to comply with the following rules:

(1) No person shall play any game other than those ball games for which the designated area has been set aside.

(2) No person shall obstruct any other person who is playing in accordance with these rules.

(3) Where exclusive use of the designated area has been granted to a person or group of persons by the Council for a specified period, no other person shall play in that area during that period.

(4) Subject to paragraph (5), where the designated area is already in use by any person, any other person wishing to play in that area must seek their permission to do so.

(5) Except where they have been granted exclusive use of the designated area for more than two hours by the Council, any person using that area shall vacate it if they have played continuously for two hours or more and any other person wishes to use that area.

(6) No person shall play in the designated area when a notice has been placed in a conspicuous position by the Council prohibiting play in that area.

These Model Byelaws should be read in conjunction with guidance notes for Model Byelaws Set 5.

MODEL BYELAWS – SET 5

[Name of Council]

BYELAWS FOR PROMENADES

ARRANGEMENT OF BYELAWS

1. Interpretation
2. [Application]
3. [Application]
4. [Application]
5. Cycling
6. Motor vehicles
7. Trading
8. Skateboarding, etc [to prohibit skateboarding, etc [except in certain areas of the promenade]]
9. Skateboarding, etc [to prohibit dangerous or nuisance skateboarding, etc]
10. Kites and kite-buggies
11. Protection of flower beds and planting
12. Unauthorised erection of structures
13. Removal of signs and structures
14. Interference with life-saving appliances
15. Obstruction
16. Savings
17. Penalty
18. Revocation

SCHEDULE

Byelaws made under section 83 of the Public Health Acts Amendment Act 1907 by the *insert name of Council* for the prevention of danger, obstruction, or annoyance to persons using the esplanades or promenades.

General interpretation

1. In these byelaws:

Select from the following list only terms to be used in the model byelaws which the Council proposes to adopt:

"the Council" means *insert name of Council*;

"designated" in relation to a route or area means set aside for a specified purpose, the route or area and the purpose to be indicated by notices placed in a conspicuous position;

"invalid carriage" means a vehicle, whether mechanically propelled or not,

(a) the unladen weight of which does not exceed 150 kilograms,

(b) the width of which does not exceed 0.85 metres, and

which has been constructed or adapted for use for the carriage of a person suffering from a disability, and used solely by such a person;

"promenade" means [name of promenade/each of the esplanades and promenades described in the Schedule to these byelaws];

"motor vehicle" means a mechanically propelled vehicle other than an invalid carriage;

"self-propelled vehicle" means a vehicle other than a cycle, invalid carriage or pram which is propelled by the weight or force of one or more persons skating, sliding or riding on the vehicle or by one or more other persons pulling or pushing the vehicle.

Application

Councils should adopt ONE of model byelaws 2, 3 and 4

Byelaws apply to all promenades in the area

2. These byelaws apply to all of the promenades within the District of *insert name of local authority area.*

Byelaws only apply to one promenade [or only part of a promenade]

3. These byelaws apply to *insert name or description of promenade* [between *describe area by reference to physical* landmarks].

Byelaws apply to several promenades

4. These byelaws apply to the promenades and esplanades listed in the Schedule.

Cycling

5. (1) No person shall without reasonable excuse ride a cycle on the promenade except where there is a right of way for cycles [or a designated route for cycles].

   (2) Where cycling is permitted on any part of the promenade by byelaw 5(1) no person shall cycle [between the hours of *insert hour* and *insert hour*] [from *insert dates* inclusive] indicated by notices conspicuously displayed on the promenade.

Motor vehicles

6. No person shall without reasonable excuse drive or bring a motor vehicle or trailer onto the promenade except—

   (a) on any part of the promenade where there is a right of way for that class of vehicle; or

   (b) for the purposes of direct access to any slipway set aside by the Council for the launching or recovery of any boat or vessel.

Trading

Nuisance or obstruction caused by sale of goods or touting

7. No person shall—

(a) sell or hawk any article or any food or drink;

(b) advertise or solicit custom for any service; or

(c) distribute handbills, circulars or advertisements,

in such a manner as to cause obstruction or annoyance to any person on the promenade.

Skateboarding, etc.

To prohibit skateboarding [except in certain areas of the promenade]

8. No person shall skate, slide or ride on rollers, skateboards or other self-propelled vehicles on the promenade [except in a designated area].

To prohibit dangerous or nuisance skateboarding

9. No person shall skate, slide or ride on rollers, skateboards or other self-propelled vehicles on the promenade in such a manner as to cause danger or give reasonable grounds for annoyance to other persons using the promenade.

Kites and kite-buggies

10. No person shall on the promenade fly any kite or ride or drive any vehicle powered by a kite in such a manner as to cause danger, nuisance or annoyance to any other person on the promenade.

Protection of flower beds and planting

11. No person shall walk on or ride over—

(a) any flower bed, shrub or plant;

(b) any ground in the course of preparation as a flower bed or for the growth of any tree, shrub or plant; or

(c) any area of the promenade set aside by the Council for

the renovation of turf or for other landscaping purposes and indicated by a notice conspicuously displayed.

Unauthorised erection of structures

12. No person shall without the consent of the Council erect any barrier, post, ride or swing, building or any other structure on the promenade.

13. No person shall, without reasonable excuse, remove from or displace any barrier, post or seat or any part of any structure or ornament or any notice or flag displayed by or on behalf of the Council or any other competent authority on the promenade.

Interference with life-saving appliances

14. No person shall, except in case of emergency, remove from or displace any life-saving appliance provided by or on behalf of the Council or other competent authority on the promenade.

Obstruction

15. No person shall on the promenade—

   (a) obstruct any officer of the Council in the proper execution of his duties;

   (b) obstruct any person carrying out an act which is necessary to the proper execution of a contract with the Council.

Savings

16. It shall not be an offence under these byelaws for an officer of the Council to do anything necessary to the proper execution of his duty or for any person acting in accordance with a contract with the Council to do anything necessary to the proper execution of that contract.

Penalty

17. Every person who shall offend against any of these byelaws shall be liable on summary conviction to a fine not exceeding level 2 on the standard scale.

Revocation

18. The byelaws relating to the promenade which were made by *insert name of council* on *insert date* and confirmed by *insert name of confirming authority* on *insert date of confirmation* are revoked.

SCHEDULE

The promenades and esplanades referred to in byelaw [4] are as follows:

COUNCILS SHOULD DOWNLOAD THIS SET FROM THE DCLG WEBSITE AND ADAPT IT AS REQUIRED

The guidance notes for Model Byelaws Set 6 should be consulted when using these Model Byelaws.

MODEL BYELAWS – SET 6

[Name of Council]

BYELAWS FOR THE SEASHORE

ARRANGEMENT OF BYELAWS

1. Interpretation
2. [Application]
3. [Application]
4. [Application]
5. Fishing
6. Sandlines
7. Bait digging [to prohibit bait digging within a limited area]
8. Bait digging [to regulate commercial bait digging]
9. Horse riding [to regulate breaking in, etc generally]
10. Horse riding [to regulate times at which breaking in, etc is permitted]
11. Public shows and performances
12. Games [to regulate games or sports generally]
13. Games [games or sports only permitted in designated areas]
14. Trading
15. Fires
16. Parties
17. Aircraft
18. Kites and kite buggies
19. Unauthorised erection of structures

Byelaws made under section 82 of the Public Health Acts Amendment Act 1907 by *insert name of Council* for the prevention of danger, obstruction, or annoyance to persons using the seashore.

Interpretation

1. In these byelaws:

Select from the following list only terms to be used in the model byelaws which the Council proposes to adopt:

"the Council" means *insert name of Council;*

"designated area" means an area of the seashore which is set aside for a specified purpose, that area and purpose to be indicated by notices placed in a conspicuous position;

"seashore" means all that area of beach and foreshore including all steps, ramps, paths and jetties from time to time situated [above the level of low water mark of medium tides/between the level of low water mark of medium tides and the promenade];

"restricted area" means such parts of the seashore between *insert details of landmark* and *insert details of landmark* as lie above the low water mark.

Application

Councils should adopt ONE of model byelaws 2, 3 and 4 only

Byelaws to apply to all seashore in the area

2. These byelaws apply to all areas of seashore that border the [District/Borough, etc] of *insert name of local authority area.*

Byelaws to apply to one beach or part of a beach

3. These byelaws apply to *insert name or description of beach/* the area of seashore lying between *describe by reference to landmarks* on *insert name or description of beach.*

Byelaws to apply to several areas of seashore

4. These byelaws apply to the areas of the seashore listed in the Schedule.

Fishing

5. No person shall fish from the seashore in such a manner as to cause danger, obstruction or annoyance to any person using the seashore.

Sandlines

6. No sandlines shall be laid in such a position as to be likely to cause injury to any person using the seashore, and all sandlines shall be visibly marked.

Bait digging

To prohibit bait digging within a limited area

7. No person shall dig for fishing bait within the restricted area.

To regulate commercial bait digging

8. No person shall dig for fishing bait for commercial purposes except with the consent of the Council.

Horse riding

To regulate breaking in, etc generally

9. No person shall break in or ride or drive any horse or other animal on the seashore in such a manner as to cause danger or annoyance to any other person.

To regulate times at which breaking in, etc is permitted

10. No person shall break in or ride or drive any horse or other animal on the seashore on [*name days* and] between the hours of *insert times*.

Public shows and performances

11. (1) No person shall deliver any lecture, sermon or speech or perform any music, or hold any entertainment except in a designated area for such performances.

   (2) No person shall use any designated area for performances in such a manner as to cause obstruction or annoyance to any person using it for any purpose for which it has been set apart.

Games

To regulate games or sports generally

12. No person shall on the seashore play or participate in any game or sport so as to cause danger, obstruction or annoyance to any person.

Games or sports only permitted in designated areas

13. (1) Where the Council has set aside a designated area for a particular sport or game, no person shall participate in that game or sport except in the designated area.

    (2) No person shall obstruct any person from using a designated area for the purpose for which it is set aside.

Trading

14. No person shall—

    (a) sell or hawk any article or any food or drink;

    (b) advertise or solicit custom for any service; or

    (c) distribute handbills, circulars or advertisements,

    in such a manner as to cause obstruction or annoyance to any person on the seashore.

Fires

15. (1) No person shall on the seashore light a fire, or place, throw or drop a lighted match or any other thing likely to cause a fire.

    (2) Byelaw 15(1) shall not apply—

    (i) in a designated area for barbecues, to the lighting or use in such a manner as to safeguard against damage or danger of a properly constructed camping stove or barbecue in such a manner as to safeguard against damage or danger; or

    (ii) to the lighting of a fire on the seashore with the consent of the Council.

Parties

16. (1) No person shall hold a party on the seashore without the consent of the Council.

    (2) In byelaw 16(1), "party" means an event attended by 15 or more people at which music will be played.

Aircraft

17. No person shall except in cases of emergency start, take, off or land an aircraft on any part of the seashore except on such part as—

    (a) is designated by the Council for the starting, taking off or landing of aircraft; and

    (b) is licensed by the Civil Aviation Authority as an aerodrome.

Kites and kite buggies

18. No person shall on the seashore fly any kite or drive any vehicle powered by a kite in such a manner as to cause danger, nuisance or annoyance to any other person on the seashore.

Unauthorised erection of structures

19. (1) No person shall erect or place on the seashore any booths, tents, sheds, stands, stalls, shows, exhibitions, swings, roundabouts, or any other structure, whether fixed or movable, except in a designated area for such structures.

    (2) Byelaw 19(1) shall not apply to the use of personal windbreaks.

Removal of signs and structures

20. No person shall without reasonable excuse remove from the seashore or displace any barrier, post or seat or any part of any structure or ornament or any notice or flag displayed by or on behalf of the Council or any other competent authority.

Interference with life-saving appliances

21. No person shall except in case of emergency remove from the seashore or displace any life-saving appliance provided by or on behalf of the Council or any other competent authority.

Obstruction

22. No person shall on the seashore—

    (a) obstruct any officer of the Council in the proper execution of his duties;

    (b) obstruct any person carrying out an act which is necessary to the proper execution of a contract with the Council.

Savings

Savings for acts done by Council officers and contractors

23. It shall not be an offence under these byelaws for an officer of the Council to do anything necessary to the proper execution of his duty or for any person acting in accordance with a contract with the Council to do anything necessary to the proper execution of that contract.

Savings to protect rights of the Crown and, where relevant, the Duchy of Cornwall

24. Nothing in or done under these byelaws shall—

    (a) operate as a grant by or on behalf of the Crown [or the Duchy of Cornwall] as owner of the foreshore below high water mark of any estate or interest in or right over the foreshore or any part of it;

    (b) prejudice the rights and interests of the Crown [or the Duchy of Cornwall];

    (c) prevent the exercise of any public rights; or

    (d) affect any right, power or privilege legally exercisable by any person in, over and in respect of the foreshore.

Penalty

25. Any person offending against any of these byelaws shall be liable on summary conviction to a fine not exceeding level 2 on the standard scale.

Revocation of byelaws

26. The byelaws relating to the seashore which were made by *insert name* on *insert date* and confirmed by *insert name of confirming authority* on *insert date byelaws of confirmation* are revoked.

SCHEDULE
[AREAS OF SEASHORE TO WHICH BYELAWS APPLY]

INDEX

Index

Index

Index

Index

Index